LIFE OF WHITTIER.

LIFE

OF

JOHN GREENLEAF WHITTIER.

BY

W. J. LINTON.

KENNIKAT PRESS
Port Washington, N. Y./London

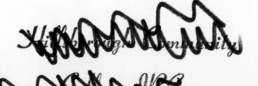

LIFE OF JOHN GREENLEAF WHITTIER

First published in 1893
Reissued in 1972 by Kennikat Press
Library of Congress Catalog Card No: 74-160768
ISBN 0-8046-1596-9

Manufactured by Taylor Publishing Company   Dallas, Texas

NOTE.

⸺•⸺

FOR most of the facts in this Memoir I am indebted
to two biographies, one by W. Sloane Kennedy,
published in 1882, the other by Francis H. Underwood,
published in 1884. Concerning the second, I have
before me the following, in Mr. Whittier's own hand,
written in 1881 :—

"My friend, F. H. Underwood, has, with my consent, and with
such aid and facilities as my friends can give him, undertaken the
preparation of a volume of which I am the subject. . . . I wish to
say that he alone has authority from me, and that he will do his
work carefully and conscientiously, and that, if his book is lacking
in interest, it will be the fault of the subject and not of the author."

Of course, the present writer is answerable for the
weaving of the story in its actual form, for the choice
of extracts, and for all expression of opinion on the
poet's work.

W. J. LINTON.

CONTENTS.

CHAPTER I.

PAGE

" The Poet of New England"; Parkman, Stedman, and Horace
Greeley on Whittier's claims to be so regarded . . 11

CHAPTER II.

The poet's genealogy ; Thomas Whittier from Southampton,
England ; the Whittier family, the Greenleafs, Husseys,
and Bachilers ; the poet born 17th or 31st December,
1807 16

CHAPTER III.

The valley of the Merrimac River in Essex County, Massachusetts; the towns of Haverhill, Amesbury, and Newburyport ; character of the scenery in the neighbourhood ;
social standing of the Whittier family ; Quaker visitors ;
the old homestead ; its building and description ; recent
appearance 21

CHAPTER IV.

The Whittier family, and guests ; Whittier's own account of his
youth and of its surroundings in his "Winter Idyll"—
" Snowbound ;" the father, mother, an Italian traveller,
Uncle Moses, Aunt Mercy, the sisters, the schoolmaster ;
Harriet Livermore and her journeys to Jerusalem and the
East 30

CHAPTER V.

Farm work and school ; the " Barefoot Boy " ; Jonathan
Plummer ; introduction to the poetry of Burns ; schooling;
early poem published in the *Free Press ;* first introduction
to its editor, William Lloyd Garrison 43

CHAPTER VI.

Goes to Academy at Haverhill, in April, 1827; first literary
days ; description of him at that date by Mrs. Thayer

PAGE

and Mrs. Pitman ; Garrison's publishing endeavours ;
Whittier's newspaper work in the *American Manufacturer*,
Haverhill Gazette, and *New England Review* ; Father
dies in June, 1831 ; " New England Legends " ; " Introduction " to Brainard's Poems ; " Moll Pitcher " ; eulogy
on Sumner 53

CHAPTER VII.

Tho Abolitionist movement ; Garrison's *Liberator* started at
the beginning of 1831 ; the American Anti-Slavery
Society ; Convention at Philadelphia ; Whittier's description of the members ; Mr. May's lecture in Haverhill ;
George Thompson ; 'Lowell's question—how a Quaker
could have got into such a hurly-burly ; Whittier's reply ;
his view of heroism ; his admiration of Milton's last days . 61

CHAPTER VIII.

Esteem of Whittier's fellow citizens despite his Abolitionism ;
the poet as politician ; appointed as representative in State
Legislature in 1835 and 1836 ; " Mogg Megone " ; " Adams'
Letters to his Constituents " ; Pamphlet from Harriet
Martineau ; the *Pennsylvania Freeman ;* the office of
the *Freeman* and the Pennsylvanian Anti-Slavery Hall
sacked and burned in May, 1838 ; Southern approval of
the outrage ; attitude of the main Quaker body ; Whittier's
position in the Society ; newspaper writing, lecturing,
and political work ; at Lowell in 1844 ; the Mexican
War ; Whittier greatly opposed to it ; the " Voices of
Freedom " ; their intensity ; " Stanzas " on the *Liberator ;*
" The Pastoral Letter " ; on " British Emancipation " ;
neither Conservatives nor Abolitionists fair critics of the
" Voices " ; the fierceness of tone justified by impending
danger ; the " Pine Tree " 73

CHAPTER IX.

Literary work from 1832 to 1847 ; " Moll Pitcher " ; the *New
England Magazine ;* its editors and contributors ; list of
Whittier's contributions, and to the *Democratic Review ;*
the " Supernaturalism of New England " ; writings in the
*North Star, Boston Pearl, New York Mirror, Emanci-
pator, Liberator, Haverhill Gazette ;* " Lays of Home " ;
more " Voices of Freedom " ; " Cassandra Southwick " ;
" Memories " ; suggestions of an early love ; " My
Summer with Dr. Singletary " ; Whittier's identification
with the Merrimac River ; description of the river's course
and geological formation ; parts of the country most
known by the poet ; ballads of " St. John " and the
" Funeral Tree of the Sokokis " ; wider sympathies . 89

CONTENTS.

CHAPTER X.

The *National Era* established in 1847; Whittier as assistant
editor; more than eighty of his poems in it between 1847
and 1859; "Uncle Tom's Cabin" appears in the *National
Era* in 1850; "Barclay of Ury"; "Ichabod"; scattering
of his poems; prose work in the *Era;* "Old Portraits";
"Literary Recreations"; "Margaret Smith's Journal" . 101

CHAPTER XI.

Editions of the poems; that of Mussey in 1849; valuable for
its notes; "Songs of Labour." Editions of 1852, '53, '54,
and '57; Whittier's mother dies in 1857; other deaths
in the Whittier family; life of poet at this time uneventful;
Explanatory notes on the poems; the "Hero"; "Ran-
toul"; "Calef in Boston"; the "Branded Hand"; "To
Faneuil Hall"; "To Massachusetts"; the "Pine Tree";
the "Pæan"; "Lines to a Southern Statesman";
"Leggett's Monument"; his verse never adulatory;
occasions for poems in the struggle for Kansas and Nebraska; "Voices of Freedom" again; the "Pass of the
Sierra"; the "Kansas Emigrants"; the "Swan's
Marsh"; the "Burial of Barbour"; lines "to A. K.";
"Mary Garvin"; "Summer by the Lakeside"; the
"Last Walk in Autumn"; "My Namesake"; Bryant,
Longfellow, Emerson, and Lowell, in the anti-slavery
movement; the bulk of the anti-slavery poetry; the
Whittier edition of 1857; the *Atlantic Monthly* started;
his allowance of other judgments; "Home Ballads";
notes to poems 113

CHAPTER XII.

John Brown; his settling in Kansas; his warfare with the pro-
slavery raiders from Missouri; the fight at Ossawatomie;
description and character; his twenty men in Kansas;
he gets possession of the armoury at Harper's Ferry, in
October, 1850, but cannot hold it; his band slain or taken
prisoners; himself a prisoner; Whittier's expression of
sympathy checked by his principles condemning armed
action; letter to Mrs. Child; lines on John Brown's
action on his way to the gallows; the poet's attitude
towards the war between the North and South in 1861
and 1862; the thirtieth anniversary of the American
Anti-Slavery Society; Whittier's letter to Garrison; the
end of slavery proclaimed 129

CHAPTER XIII.

Poems—not of war, but written during the war; the war over,
he devotes himself to his art; "Snowbound, a Winter
Idyll," the most perfect of the poet's works, published in

PAGE

1865; the "Tent on the Beach"; some national lyrics; "Laus Deo"; the "Peace Autumn"; other poems, lyrics, and ballads; "In School Days"; the "Pennsylvania Pilgrim," with a prefatory plea for the Quakers; the "Sisters"; "Hazel Blossoms," with poems by Elizabeth Whittier, published in 1875; "In a Sea-Dream"; "Mabel Martin"; the "Henchman"; the "Vision of Echard"; the "Witch of Wenham"; "Sunset on the Bearcamp"; "In the Old South"; other poems; hymns; "Children's Poems"; "Three Centuries of Song"; "To Oliver Wendell Holmes"; last words and last days; he dies on the 7th of December, 1892; funeral; his legacies 140

CHAPTER XIV.

His place as a poet; at first the preacher; some carelessnesses; lack of early musical training; poetic hopes given up to the cause of freedom; his own expression of this; yet something gained; compared with Poe; and Wordsworth; "Telling the Bees"; his descriptive poetry characterised by Stoddard; "A Dream of Summer"; personal poems; Stoddard's further criticism; Whittier a natural balladist; the strong human element in him; "Barbara Frietchie"; "Floyd Ireson" 166

CHAPTER XV.

Criticism continued; Mr. Wasson in the *Atlantic Monthly;* Whittier's Semitic appearance and character; a real life; the poet and the man one; Quakerism and Puritanism; his devotion to Freedom the choice of a true man; his the rare power of creating homely beauty; Stedman on the early influences of his life; Nature learned from herself; brief review of his life and estimate of his verse; conclusion 183

INDEX 199

LIFE OF WHITTIER.

CHAPTER I.

THE Poet of New England (so called by the historian Parkman), the Prophet-bard of America, the Quaker Poet—these titles fairly and truly mark the literary status of John Greenleaf Whittier. Add to them his own sincere and characteristic avowal, " I set a higher value on my name as appended to the Anti-Slavery Declaration of 1833 than on the title-page of any book," and we have fair sight not only of the poet, but of the man.

The Poet of New England:—"His genius drew its nourishment from her soil; his pages are the mirror of her outward nature and the strong utterance of her inward life." These were Parkman's words at a gathering in honour of Whittier. "The gloss of the sentiment," writes Stedman, in his "Poets of America" (1885), "belonged to the occasion; its analysis is specifically correct, and this with full recognition of Whittier's most famous kinsmen in birth and song. The distinction has been well made that the national poet is not always the chief

poet of a nation.   As a poet of New England Whittier
had little competition from the bookish Longfellow,
except in the latter's sincere feeling for the eastern sea
and shore, and his artistic handling of the courtlier
legends of the province.   He certainly found a compeer
in Lowell, whose dialect idylls prove that only genius is
needed to enable a scholar turned farmer to extract the
richest products of a soil; and the lyric fervour of Lowell's
odes is our most imaginative expression of that New
England sentiment which has extended itself, an ideal
influence, with the movement of its inheritors to the
farthest West.   Emerson, on his part, has volatilised the
essence of New England thought into wreaths of spiritual
beauty.   Yet Mr. Parkman, than whom no scholar is less
given to looseness of expression, terms Whittier *the* poet
of New England, as if by eminence, and, I think, with
justice.   The title is based on apt recognition that we
look to the people at large for the substance of national
or sectional traits.   The base, not the peak, of the pyra-
mid determines its bearings.   There is, to be sure, as
much human nature in the mansion as in the cottage, in
the study or the drawing-room as in the shop and field.
But just as we call those *genre* canvases, whereon are
painted idylls of the fireside, the roadside, and the farm,
pictures of 'real life,' so we find the true gauge of popular
feeling in songs that are dear to the common people and
true to their unsophisticated life and motive."

To continue with Stedman: "Here we confront the
statement that the six Eastern States were not and are
not America—not the nation, but a section, the New
Englanders seeming almost a race by themselves.   But

what a section! And what a people, when we take into account, superadded to their genuine importance, a self-dependence ranking with that of the Scots or Gascons! As distinct a people, in their way, as Mr. Cable's Creoles, old or new. Go by rail along the eastern coast, and note the nervous, wiry folk that crowd the stations; their eager talk, their curious scrutiny of ordinary persons and incidents, make it easy to believe that the trait chosen by Sprague for the subject of his didactic poem still is a chief motor of New England's progress, and not unjustly its attribute by tradition. This hive of individuality has sent out swarms and scattered its ideas like pollen throughout the northern belt of our States. As far as these have taken hold, modified by change and experience, New England stands for the nation, and her singer for the national poet. In their native unadulterated form they pervade the verse of Whittier. It is notable that the sons of the Puritans should take their songs from a Quaker; yet how far unlike, except in the doctrine of non-resistance, were the Puritans and Quakers of Endicott's time? To me they seem grounded in the same inflexible ethics of all mankind. Time and culture have tempered the New England virtues; the Eastern frugality, independence, propagandism, have put on a more attractive aspect; a sense of beauty has been developed—the mental recognition of it finally granted to a northern race, who still lack the perfect flexibility and grace observable wherever that sense comes by nature and directs the popular conscience. As for the rural inhabitants of New England, less changed by travel and accomplishments, we know what they were and are

—among them none more affectionate, pious, resolute than Whittier, beyond doubt their representative poet.

"He belongs, moreover, and hence the point of the incident first related,[1] to the group, now rapidly disappearing, of which Horace Greeley was a conspicuous member, and to an epoch that gave its workers little time for over-refinement, Persian apparatus, and the cultivation of æsthetics. That group of scarred and hardy speakers, journalists, agitators, felt that he was of them, and found his song revealing the highest purpose of their boisterous, unsentimental careers. These men, like all men who do not retrograde, had an ideal. This he expressed in measures that moved them, and whose perfection they had no thought or faculty of questioning. Many of them came from obscure and rural homes, and to read his verse was to recall the scent of the clover and apple-bloom, to hear again the creak of the well-pole, the rattle of the bars in the lane—the sights and freshness of youth passing for a moment, a vision of peace, over their battle-field. They needed, also, their own pibroch and battle-cry, and this his song rang out; their determination was in it, blended with the tenderness from which such men are never wholly free.

"His ultimate reputation, then, will be inseparable from that of his section and its class. He may not hold

---

[1] A story that, shortly after the close of the American civil war, a group of prominent men met together, and the question arose in conversation, Who was the best American poet? Horace Greeley, one of the party, replied with the name of Whittier, and his judgment was instantly approved by the various practical, not poetical, men present.

it as one of those whose work appeals to all times and races, and whose orb is so refined as to be the model of after poets. But he was the singer of what was not an empty day, and of a section whose movement became that of a nation, and whose purpose in the end was grandly consummated. We already see, and the future will see it more clearly, that no party ever did a vaster work than his party ; that he, like Hampden and Milton, is a character not produced in common times; that no struggle was more momentous than that which preceded our Civil War, no question ever affected the destinies of a great people more vitally than the anti-slavery issue as urged by its promoters. Neither Greece nor Rome, not even England, the battle-ground of Anglo-Saxon liberty, has supplied a drama of more import than that in which the poets and other heroes of our Civil Reformation played their parts."

Whittier was the bard of a great historic time.

CHAPTER II.

I N the year 1638 one Thomas Whittier, or Whittle (names in those days of uncertain spelling being written with much variety), came from Southampton, England, to New England,—the only noteworthy circumstance, says his poet descendant, that was connected with his coming being that he brought with him a hive of bees. This Thomas Whittier was born in 1620, his mother, says Mr. Kennedy, probably a sister of John and Henry Rolfe, with the former of whom he came to America. He married Ruth Green, and lived at first in Salisbury, Massachusetts, and afterwards in Newbury, both towns situated on the Merrimac River. In 1650 he removed to Haverhill, on the same river, where he was admitted as a freeman, but not until the 22nd of May, 1666. Freemen—the voting class—were admitted by the General Court, not by the towns; this may account for the delay in his admission, supposing that his opinions in regard to religious liberty did not accord with those of the ruling power. Various minutes in the town records attest the esteem in which he was held, but it would seem that though he remained in fellowship with the Church at Haverhill, he inclined at heart, and somewhat openly also, to the Quaker tenets.

In those days, says the historian of Haverhill, during the Indian wars, it was usual for the nearest neighbours to sleep together, their houses fortified, or to take shelter at night with the garrison; but such protection was constantly refused by Whittier. He kept his house unguarded and without palisades, and carried no arms. The Indians frequently visited him, and the family would hear them in the stillness of the evening whispering beneath the windows, and sometimes could see them peeping in. Whittier always treated them civilly and hospitably, and neither he nor any of his family or descendants were ever molested by them. Yet for many years houses were burned, and men, women, and children were tomahawked and scalped in all the river towns.

Thomas Whittier died at Haverhill on the 28th of November, 1696. He had ten children, the youngest of whom, Joseph, was the great-grandfather of the poet. Joseph had nine children, among them a second Joseph, the poet's grandfather. This second Joseph married Sarah Greenleaf, of Newbury, by whom he had eleven children, the tenth child, John, the poet's father. The poet's mother was Abigail Hussey, a daughter of Joseph Hussey, of Somersworth (now Rollinsford), New Hampshire, a town on the Piscataqua River, which forms the boundary between New Hampshire and Maine. John and Abigail Whittier had four children— Mary, John, Matthew, and Elizabeth. The second-born, John Greenleaf, our poet, referring to all the books, was born on the 17th of December, 1807, and his birthday has been kept accordingly. Yet I have a letter from him in his own handwriting, bearing date "13, 9ᵐᵒ, 1875," in which, answering my inquiry, he writes: "My birthday was the very last of the year 1807." However, whether he was born on the 17th or the 31st is not of very much consequence.

The name of Whittier continually appears in important documents signed with the names of other and chief citizens of Haverhill; and the family were evidently well esteemed by their neighbours, although not exempt from some consequences of their religious belief. For instance, when the citizens built a new meeting-house, in 1699, they peremptorily refused to allow the Quakers to worship in it, although the Quakers were taxed for its support. It was not until 1774 that an Act was passed by the State Legislature of Massachusetts relieving Dissenters from taxation for the support of the State religion.

The ancestors of Sarah Greenleaf, the poet's paternal grandmother, are believed to have been Huguenots, who left France at the close of the sixteenth century and found refuge in England. Edmund Greenleaf, the ancestor of the American family, was born in the parish of Brixham, Devonshire, near Torbay, in about the year 1600. He was by trade a silk dyer, and came to Newbury, Massachusetts, in 1635. The name is possibly an English rendering of the French *Feuillevert*, Whittier himself countenancing this in the following lines :—

> "The name the Gallic exile bore,
> St. Malo! from thy ancient mart,

Became upon our Western shore
Greenleaf for Feuillevert."

The name of another Greenleaf, contemporary with
Edmund, is found as that of a lieutenant in Cromwell's
army. A later relative was Simon Greenleaf, Law
Professor at Harvard University from 1833 to 1845, a
writer also of works legal and religious, and recorded as
"one of the most spiritually minded of men." His son
James married Mary Longfellow, the sister of the
Cambridge poet.

In a note addressed to the New England Historical
and Genealogical Society, Whittier writes : " On my
mother's side my grandfather was Joseph Hussey, of
Somersworth, New Hampshire, my grandmother, Mercy
Evans, of Berwick, Maine." In 1630 one Christopher
Hussey came from Dorking, in England, to Lynn,
Massachusetts. He had married in Holland, Theodate,
a daughter of the Rev. Stephen Bachiler (or Batchelder),
a Puritan minister, who had fled to Holland to escape
from persecution in England. There is a tradition that
Bachiler would not allow his daughter to marry Hussey
unless the young man embraced the Puritan faith. His
love was so great that he consented, and came with his
bride to America, where, two years later, his father-in-
law followed him. Stephen Bachiler came to Lynn in
1632, with six persons, relatives and friends, who had
belonged to his church in Holland, and with them
established a little independent church at Lynn. Recorded dates show that both he and his son-in-law came
to Hampton in 1639, the Hampton authorities having in

the previous year made to Mr. Bachiler and Mr. Hussey each a grant of three hundred acres of land, to induce them to settle there. How or when they became Quakers does not appear; but in Savage's " Genealogical Dictionary " it is stated that as early as 1688 one John Hussey, of Hampton, was a preacher of that persuasion in Newcastle, Delaware. The mother of the poet was a devoted adherent of the Society of Friends; a person of deep and tender religious nature. An excellent oil portrait of her hung in the little parlour of Whittier's house at Amesbury. The head is inclined graciously to one side, and the face wears that expression of ineffable tranquillity which is always a witness to Quaker ancestry. In the picture her garments are of smooth and immaculate drab. One reason why she removed to Amesbury, in 1840, was that she might be near the little Friends' meeting-house in that town.

So much of genealogy is of importance, as showing the stock from which our poet sprung, accounting for his inheritance of faith and sturdiness. Blood, bone, and sinew, body and soul, his make was of those who must resist oppression and wrong, and stand heroically in the van of the great world-fight for truth.

CHAPTER III.

O F the locality in which the child Whittier was born, and of his boyhood's immediate influences and surroundings, something now has to be said. His birthplace was a lonely farmhouse in the valley of the Merrimac, about three miles north-east of Haverhill, in Essex county, Massachusetts, a little town settled in 1640 by twelve men from Newbury and Ipswich, eighteen miles east of Lowell and thirty-two miles north-west of Boston. In 1870 the population was thirteen thousand, the chief employment of the inhabitants the manufacturing of boots and shoes. To strangers, says one of Whittier's biographers, Mr. Kennedy, "the hilly old county of Essex wears a somewhat bleak and Scotian aspect; but it is fertile in poetical resources, and the tillers of its glebe are passionately attached to its blue hills and sunken dales, its silver rivers and winding roads, umbrageous towns and thrifty homes." The "bleak and Scotian" seem in some sort to refer to the birthplace of Burns, near Ayr, bleak enough in its flat unpicturesqueness; but the valley of the Merrimac, with its "silver rivers, umbrageous towns and winding roads," requires a richer comparison.

The Indian name for Haverhill was Pentucket, the appellation of a tribe of the Pennacooks once dwelling on its site. The town is built partly on the adjoining hills and partly on the river-terrace of the Merrimac, which, after a southerly course from the White Mountains, through great part of New Hampshire, turns suddenly eastward on entering Massachusetts, a few miles above Lowell. Down to the sea, some seventeen miles from Haverhill, winds the beautiful river, with the deep-shaded old town of Newburyport at its mouth. A little more than half way down lies Amesbury, just where the winding Powow joins the Merrimac, not before its nixies and river-horses have been compelled to put their shoulders to the wheels of several huge cotton-mills that lift their ugly bulk out of the very centre of the town. A horse railroad connects Amesbury with Newburyport. Midway the road crosses the Merrimac by way of Deer Island's connecting bridges,—Deer Island wild and rough, with a single house upon it.

Nearing Newburyport, coming from Amesbury, you see the river widening into an estuary, and bordered by wide and intensely green salt meadows. Large vessels lie at the wharves, a "gundelow," with lateen sail, creeps slowly down the current; the draw of the railroad bridge is perhaps opening for the passage of a tug, and out at sea, athwart the river's mouth—

> "Long and low, with dwarf trees crown'd,
> Plum Island lies, like a whale aground,
> A stone's toss over the narrow sound."

Far off to the left lie Salisbury and Hampton beaches, "low green prairies of the sea," celebrated in Whittier's poems, "Hampton Beach," and the "Tent on the Beach."

Standing on the sand-ridge by the beach, you have before you the washing surf, and miles on miles of level sand, rimmed with creeping silver water-lace, overhung here and there by thinnest powdery mist. Out at sea the waves are tossing their salt-threaded manes or flinging the sunlight from their supple coats, while at evening you see far away to the north-east the revolving light of the Isles of Shoals.

Landward your gaze sweeps the beautiful salt meadows and rests on the woods beyond, or reaches still farther to the steeples of Newburyport. On the whole, and before the days of huge cotton-mills and railroads, the valley of the Merrimac from Haverhill to the sea must have had beauty enough to charm the heart of a poet, and fill him, as Whittier's descriptive poems well evidence, with images of poetic interest.

Along the winding road leading from Haverhill to the Whittier farm,—a road described in the poem "Snow-bound,"—a walk of one mile brings you to Kenoza Lake, formerly known as Great Pond. From a hill overlooking the lake the eye sweeps the horizon in every direction to a distance of from fifty to a hundred miles. Far off to the north-west rise bluely the three peaks of Menadnock. Nearer, in the same direction, the towns of Atkinson and Strafford whiten the hill-sides, while southward, through a cleft in the hills, one catches a glimpse of the smoky city of Lawrence.

Two other lakes besides Kenoza lie in the immediate neighbourhood: Round Lake and Lake Saltonstall. Kenoza is the lake on which Whittier used to boat and fish; and its present name (meaning Pickerel) was given by him. It lies in a bowl-shaped depression, the country thereabout seeming to be made up of huge earth-bowls, here hollowed, there turned bottom upward to make hills. No prettier, quieter, lovelier lake, writes enthusiastically Mr. Kennedy, exists than Kenoza, "a pure and spotless mirror, reflecting in its cool translucent depths the rosy clouds of morning and of evening, the silver-azure tint of day, the gliding boat, the green meadow-grasses, and the massy foliage of the terraced pines and cedars that sweep upward from its waters in stately pomp, rank over rank, to meet the sky. Here, in one quarter of the lake, the surface is only wrinkled by the tiniest wavelets or crinkles; yonder, near another portion of its irregularly picturesque shore, a thousand white sun-butterflies seem dancing on the surface, and the loveliest wind-dapples curve and gleam. Along the shore are sweet wild roses interpleached, and flower-de-luce, and yellow water-lilies. In such a circular earth-bowl the faintest sounds are easily heard across the water. Far off you hear the cheery cackle of a hen; in the meadows the singing of insects, the chattering of blackbirds, and the cry of the peewee; and the ring of the woodman's axe floats in rippling echoes over the water." What more could a rural poet want?

The two miles of road between Lake Kenoza and the old Whittier homestead form a lonely stretch, passing between high hills rolled back on either side in wolds

that show against the sky. The homestead stands at
the junction of the main road to Amesbury and a cross-
road to Plaistow. It is as wild and lonely a spot as
Carlyle's Craigenputtock, the hills shutting out all around,
so that there is absolutely no prospect in any direction,
and no other house in sight in this green sunken pocket
of the inland hills,—fit place for the nurture of a poet of
home affections.

The place of the Whittier homestead may not be
beautiful in a painter's sense; but the scene is quiet,
near to original nature, unmodernised, as if a survival
from a past century : a scene in which we might look to
meet the steeple-hatted farmer, in woollen hose and
doublet, following his team a-field; to see the matron
in her coif, with a kerchief over her shoulders, sitting by
the door at her spinning-wheel; the daughters hanging
festoons of sliced apples to dry; the boys tending cattle
in the lush meadows; with birds and squirrels and wood-
chucks skulking, scarce afraid of being disturbed in their
lonely haunts.

The land is only moderately fertile, and could never
have been the source of wealth to the most laborious
cultivator. In the town assessment for 1798 the farm
stands as the joint property of the poet's father, John
Whittier, and his two brothers, Joseph and Moses, and is
rated at $200 (or £40), much below value, for when, in
1806, Joseph married and removed to Maine, his share
was bought by John for $600. This sum was borrowed;
and even the interest was felt as a burden. The debt
remained during the buyer's life, and was only cleared
off by his son.

Not that the family are to be considered as poor folk. Money was scarce, but the household had good supply from the farm and from the river; the field of flax and the fleeces of the flock, spun and woven at home, gave clothing; and surplus wood, nuts, and grain, and other farm produce, helped to balance the modest expenditure at the country store. The position was much the same as that, in the England of those days, of a small Cumberland "statesman" among the hills, a position of at least self-support, sufficiency for material wants, and independence. The testimony of neighbours speaks of the family as well-to-do folk; and much esteemed in Haverhill, where the father was frequently in the public service and intimate with the most important citizens. Visits of travelling friends broke also the quiet monotony of the home. The New England Quakers were widely scattered, and there were no railroads to forward them in their attendance on the annual meeting at Newport, in Rhode Island; so that on their several days' journey thither they had to depend on the hospitality of friends. It is told that on one occasion no fewer than sixteen of such guests slept at the Whittier house, probably some of them housed in the barn. Among notable visitors was William Forster, the father of W. E. Forster, the Secretary for Ireland.

Great-great-grandfather Thomas had settled upon a tract of land in the eastern part of Haverhill, about three miles from the centre, and built for his family a log-house, in which he lived for many years. Afterwards, about 1688, he erected a large and solidly framed house, half a mile north-west from the first, which became the home of his descendants, and in which the poet was born. The house was of two stories in front, the rear sloping down to a single story. The rear was raised, and the house otherwise improved, in 1801, by the poet's father.

The house stood a little off the road. Between the front door and the road rises a grassy, wooded bank, at the foot of which flows a little brook mentioned in "Snowbound," as, when winter-covered—

> "We minded that the sharpest ear
> The buried brooklet could not hear;
> The music of whose liquid lip
> Had been to us companionship,
> And in our lonely life had grown
> To have an almost human tone."

Across the road was the barn. The house is very plain, and not large. Entering at the front door, you are in a small entry with a steep, quaint narrow staircase. On the right is the parlour where Whittier wrote; on the left, a low room in which he was born, and in which his father and an uncle Moses died—a room about fourteen feet square, with three windows. The house has been altered in late years; but within it remains substantially the same as in the period spoken of in Whittier's "Snowbound." New doors and window sashes, and fresh paint, have somewhat modernised its outer appearance; but some ancient carpentry remains, and, within a few years from now, there were still in use the quaint iron door-handles, latches, and hinges, which Puritan smiths hammered out two centuries ago. "The glass in the windows" (writes Mr. Underwood in 1884), "is modern, except a few panes in the kitchen and chambers. The sturdy chimney has been newly topped; but its antiquity is evident when its huge mass is seen in the open space of the large back chamber. One sees that the chimney was the central idea of a new settler's home. The kitchen fireplace, once broad enough to admit benches on either side, has now been narrowed by rows of bricks, thereby closing a curious cave of an oven buried in the recess. Though reduced in size by a partition, it is yet a cosy room, with the cupboard set in one side, where the pewter plates and platters were ranged, still showing on the wall the circle worn by the old brass warming-pan.

"The square front rooms are unchanged. The marks of their century, strength and simplicity, are upon every part of the work; the outer beams, which a man of fair height can touch with an upraised hand, are fifteen inches square, and as firm as when laid. The wainscots and floors are well preserved.

"At one end of the kitchen was a bedroom known as the mother's room; but it was in the west front room that our poet saw the light. The small chamber over-head is the one he occupied when a boy. A flight of well-worn steps leads up to it from the kitchen. Above are the time-stained rafters and the boards pierced with nail-points, which used to glisten liked powdered stars on frosty mornings. Here it was, as the poet has told us, that, on stormy nights,

" ' We heard the loosen'd clap-boards tost,
    The board-nails snapping in the frost;
    And on us, through the unplaster'd wall,
    Felt the light-sifted snow-flakes fall.'

" If readers can recall the parts of this description, and look upon the old farmhouse from a proper point without, it will be seen that, if there were once more a garden in front, a tall well-sweep at the left, the barn and shed in the rear, and if the oaks on every side were renewed, sturdier, thicker, nearer, the place would be once more as it was when Whittier was a boy."

CHAPTER IV.

AND who were the boy's housemates? The sturdy father, a rough but good, kind-hearted man, deeply religious and decisive, who in early days had led an adventurous life in the vast forest which then stretched from southern New Hampshire to Canada. In "Snowbound" we have hints of him as, in retrospective talk beside the kitchen fire—

> " Our father rode again his ride
>   On Memphremagog's wooded side ;
>   Sat down again to moose and vamp
>   In trapper's hut and Indian camp ;
>   Lived o'er the old idyllic ease
>   Beneath St. François' hemlock trees.
>   Again for him the moonlight shone
>   On Norman cap and bodiced zone ;
>   Again he heard the violin play,
>   Which led the village dance away,
>   And mingled in its merry whirl
>   The grandam and the laughing girl.
>   Or, nearer home, our steps he led

Where Salisbury's level meadows spread
Mile-wide as flies the laden bee;
Where merry mowers, hale and strong,
Swept scythe on scythe their swathes along
The low green prairies of the sea.
We shared the fishing off Boar's Head,
And round the rocky Isles of Shoals,
The hake-broil on the drift-wood coals,
The chowder on the sand-beach made,
Dipp'd by the hungry, steaming hot,
With spoons of clam-shell from the pot.
We heard the tales of witchcraft old,
And dream and sign and marvel told
To sleepy listeners as they lay
Stretch'd idly on the salted hay,
Adrift along the winding shores,
When favouring breezes deign'd to blow
The square sail of the gundelow,
And idle lay the useless oars."

In later time, on every First-day, the father's one-horse shay was to be seen on the six miles towards the meeting-house at Amesbury, there being no Friends meeting-house at Haverhill.

The mother's nature appears to have been deeply emotional and religious, pure, chastened, and sweet, lovable and kind-hearted, the good Quaker character-istics. "On one occasion" (it is Whittier who speaks) "on my return from the field at evening, I was told that a foreigner had asked for lodging during the night, but, that influenced by his dark, repulsive appearance, my

mother had very reluctantly refused his request.   I found
her by no means satisfied with her decision.   'What if
a son of mine was in a strange land?' she inquired, self-
reproachfully.   Greatly to her relief, I volunteered to go
in pursuit of the wanderer, and, taking a cross path over
the fields, soon overtook him. He had just been rejected
at the house of our nearest neighbour; and was standing
in a state of dubious perplexity in the street.   His looks
quite justified my mother's suspicions.   He was an
olive-complexioned, black-bearded Italian, with an eye
like a live coal, such a face as perchance looks out on the
traveller in the passes of the Abruzzi, one of those bandit
visages which Salvator has painted. With some difficulty
I gave him to understand my errand, when he over-
whelmed me with thanks, and joyfully followed me back.
He took his seat with us at the supper-table; and,
when we were all gathered round the hearth that cold
autumnal evening, he told us, partly by words, and partly
by gestures, the story of his life and misfortunes; amused
us with descriptions of the grape-gatherings and festivals
of his sunny clime; edified my mother with a recipe for
making bread of chestnuts; and in the morning, when
after breakfast his dark sullen face lighted up, and his
fierce eyes moistened with grateful emotion as in his own
silvery Tuscan accent he poured out his thanks, we
marvelled at the fears which had so nearly closed our
doors against him; and, as he departed, we all felt that
he had left with us the blessing of the poor.

"It was not often that, as in the above instance, my
mother's prudence got the better of her charity.   The
regular 'old stragglers' regarded her as an unfailing

friend; and the sight of her plain cap was to them an assurance of forthcoming creature comforts."

A woman to be loved; thus again by the poet introduced to us at the family hearth in those prisoned hours of the snowstorm :—

"Our mother, while she turn'd her wheel,
  Or ran the new-knit stocking-heel,
  Told how the Indian hordes came down
  At midnight on Cochecho town,
  And how her own great-uncle bore
  His cruel scalp-mark to fourscore;
  Recalling, in her fitting phrase,
  So rich and picturesque and free,
  (The common unrhymed poetry
  Of simple life and country ways)
  The story of her early days.
  She made us welcome to her home;
  Old hearths grew wide to give us room;
  We stole with her a frighten'd look
  At the grey wizard's conjuring book,
  The fame whereof went far and wide
  Through all the simple country side;
  We heard the hawks at twilight play,
  The boat-horn on Piscataqua,
  The loon's weird laughter far away;
  We fish'd her little trout-brook, knew
  What flowers in wood and meadow grew,
  What sunny hillsides autumn-brown
  She climb'd to shake the ripe nuts down;
  Saw where in shelter'd cove or bay

The ducks' black squadron anchor'd lay,
And heard the wild geese calling loud
Beneath the grey November cloud.
Then, haply, with a look more grave
And soberer tone, some tale she gave
From painful Sewell's ancient tome,
Beloved in every Quaker home,
Of faith fire-wing'd by martyrdom."

    .   .   .   .   .   .

Unmarried Uncle Moses Whittier appears next in "Snowbound" as a member of the happy household : a tall, plain, sober man, less stirring than his brother John, and younger, " a man for the little folk to love," and chief comrade of the poet in his boyhood.

"Our uncle, innocent of books,
  Was rich in lore of fields and brooks,
  The ancient teachers never dumb
  Of Nature's unhoused Lyceum.
  In moons and tides and weather wise,
  He read the clouds as prophecies ;
  And foul or fair could well divine
  By many an occult hint and sign,
  Holding the cunning-warded keys
  To all the woodcraft mysteries ;
  Himself to Nature's heart so near
  That all her voices in his ear
  Of beast or bird had meanings clear ;
  Like Apollonius of old,
  Who knew the tales the sparrows told,
  Or Hermes who interpreted

What the sage cranes of Nilus said:
A simple, guileless, child-like man,
Content to live where life began;
Strong only on his native grounds,
The little world of sights and sounds
Whose girdle was the parish bounds;
Whereof his fondly partial pride
The common features magnified,
As Surrey hills to mountains grew
In White of Selborne's loving view.
He told how teal and loon he shot,
And how the eagle's eggs he got,
The feats on pond and river done,
The prodigies of rod and gun;
Till, warming with the tales he told,
Forgotten was the outside cold,
The bitter wind unheeded blew,
From ripen'd corn the pigeons flew,
The partridge drumm'd i' the wood, the mink
Went fishing down the river-brink;
In fields with bean or clover gay
The woodchuck, like a hermet grey,
Peer'd from the doorway of his cell.
The musk-rat plied the mason's trade,
And tier by tier his mud-walls laid;
And from the shagbark overhead
The grizzled squirrel dropp'd his shell.

Next the dear Aunt, whose smile of cheer
And voice in dreams I see and hear,
The sweetest woman ever Fate

Perverse denied a houshold mate,
Who lonely, homeless, not the less
Found peace in love's unselfishness,
And welcome whereso'er she went,
Whose presence seem'd the sweet out-come
And womanly atmosphere of home,—
Call'd up her girlhood memories,
The huskings and the apple-bees,
The sleigh rides and the summer sails ;
Weaving through all the poor details
And homespun warp of circumstance
A golden woof-thread of romance :
For well she kept her genial mood
And simple faith of maidenhood :
Before her still a cloud-land lay,
The mirage loom'd across her way ;
The morning dew, that dries so soon
With others, glisten'd at her noon ;
Through years of toil and soil and care,
From glossy tress to thin grey hair,
All unprofaned she held apart
The virgin fancies of the heart.
Be shame to him of woman born
Who hath for such but thought of scorn !"

The two sisters, Mary and Elizabeth, follow.

" There too our elder sister plied
   Her evening task the stand beside :
   A full, rich nature, free to trust,
   Truthful and almost sternly just,

Impulsive, earnest, prompt to act
And make her generous thought a fact,
Keeping with many a light disguise
The secret of self-sacrifice.

.   .   .

As one who held herself a part
Of all she saw, and let her heart
Against the household bosom lean,
Upon the motley-braided mat
Our youngest and our dearest sat,
Lifting her large, sweet, asking eyes,
Now bathed within the fadeless green
And holy peace of Paradise."

Very, very dear this young sister, a poet also, was to him. She was nine years younger than himself.

Two characters, not of the family, but with them shut up in the snowed-up house, are too well drawn to be unnoticed now that we are standing by the Whittier fire.

" Brisk wielder of the birch and rule,
The master of the district school
Held at the fire his favour'd place.
Its warm glow lit a laughing face,
Fresh-hued and fair, where scarce appear'd
The uncertain prophecy of beard.
He teased the mitten-blinded cat,
Play'd cross-pins on my uncle's hat,
Sang songs, and told us what befalls
In classic Dartmouth college halls.
Born the wild Northern hills among,

From whence his yeoman father wrung,
By patient toil, subsistence scant,
Not competence and yet not want,
He early gain'd the power to pay
His cheerful, self-reliant way:
Could doff at ease his scholar's gown
To peddle wares from town to town ;
Or through the long vacation's reach
In lonely woodland districts teach,
Where all the droll experience found
At stranger hearths in boarding round,
The moonlit skater's keen delight,
The sleigh drive through the frosty night,
The rustic party, with its rough
Accompaniment of blind-man's buff,
And whirling plate and forfeits paid,
His winter task a pastime made.
Happy the snow-lock'd homes wherein
He tuned his merry violin,
Or play'd the athlete in the barn,
Or held the good dame's winding yarn,
Or mirth-provoking versions told
Of classic legends rare and old,
Wherein the scenes of Greece and Rome
Had all the common-place of home,
And little seem'd at best the odds
'Twixt Yankee pedlars and old gods ;
Where Pindus-born Araxes took
The guise of any grist-mill brook,
And dread Olympus, at his will,
Became a huckleberry hill.

A careless boy that night he seem'd ;
But at his desk he had the look
And air of one who wisely schemed,
And hostage from the future took
In trainèd thought and lore of book.
Large brain'd, clear-eyed—of such as he
Shall Freedom's young apostles be.

    •   •   •   •

Another guest that winter night
Flash'd back from lustrous eyes the light.
Unmark'd by time, and yet not young,
The honey'd music of her tongue
And words of meekness scarcely told
A nature passionate and bold,
Strong, self-concentred, spurning guide,
Its milder features dwarf'd beside
Her unbent will's majestic pride.
She sat among us, at the best
A not unfear'd, half-welcome guest,
Rebuking with her cultured phrase
Our homeliness of words and ways.
A certain pard-like, treacherous grace
Sway'd the lithe limbs, and dropp'd the lash,
Lent the white teeth their dazzling flash,
And under low brows, black with night,
Ray'd out at times a dangerous light ;
The sharp heat-lightnings of her face
Presagèd ill to him whom Fate
Condemn'd to share her love or hate.
A woman tropical, intense
In thought and act, in soul and sense,

She blended in a like degree
The vixen and the devotee,
Revealing with each freak or feint
The temper of Petruchio's Kate,
The raptures of Siena's saint.
Her tapering hand and rounded wrist
Had facile power to form a fist;
The warm, dark languish of her eyes
Was never safe from wrath's surprise;
Brows saintly calm and lips devout
Knew every change of scowl and pout;
And the sweet voice had notes more high
And shrill, for social battle-cry."

This was the religious enthusiast and fanatical " pilgrim preacher," Harriet Livermore, the grand-daughter of Hon. Samuel Livermore, of Portsmouth, New Hampshire, and daughter of Hon. Edward St. Loe Livermore, from whom she is said to have inherited her temper. When Whittier was a child she taught needlework, embroidery, and common school lessons in the little schoolhouse at East Haverhill, and was a frequent guest at Farmer Whittier's. But her portrait, as drawn from the poet's recollection, must be completed :—

" Since then, what old cathedral town
Has miss'd her pilgrim staff and gown ?
What convent gate has held its lock
Against the challenge of her knock ?
Thro' Smyrna's plague-hush'd thoroughfares,
Up sea-set Malta's rocky stairs,

Grey olive slopes of hills that hem
Thy tombs and shrines, Jerusalem !
Or startling on her desert throne
The crazy Queen of Lebanon
With claims fantastic as her own,
Her tireless feet have held their way ;
And still unrestful, bow'd and grey,
She watches under Eastern skies,
With hope each day renew'd and fresh,
The Lord's quick coming in the flesh,
Whereof she dreams and prophesies."

She had at one time, says Whittier, "an idea of be-
coming a member of the Society of Friends; but an
unlucky outburst of rage, resulting in a blow, at a friend's
house in Amesbury, did not encourage us to seek her
membership." She embraced the Methodist Perfection-
ist doctrine, and maintained that she was incapable of
sinning; became an itinerant preacher, speaking at
meetings of various sects in different parts of the country ; and made three voyages to Jerusalem. At one
time we find her in Egypt, giving no end of trouble
to the American consul there. At another she is at
Jerusalem, demanding, not begging, money for the
"Great King." An American, fresh from home, offering
her notes, she threw them back disdainfully, saying that
the Great King would take only gold. She once climbed
Mount Libanus to visit Lady Hester Stanhope (the sister
of William Pitt) who had married a sheik, and so was
the possessor of some fine horses. Two were shown to
Harriet Livermore, of peculiar beauty and differing in

colour. These, said Lady Hester, are for the Great King : he will ride one, and I the other. Harriet emphatically contradicted her, declaring from her foreknowledge which the King would ride, and that she, Harriet, not Hester, would accompany Him on the other, as His bride, at His second coming.

CHAPTER V.

TO return from Lebanon to the Whittier homestead. In such a home what more could be asked for the training of a well-natured and poetic lad in noble and lovely thought? The healthiest of lives, the wholesome farm-life, with such indoors influences, was fit mould for poet or hero, for the making of a strong and good man. Doubtless he took his share of farm work, so far as boyish capability allowed, constantly employed when not at school. "At an early age," he tells us, " I was set to work on the farm and doing errands for my mother, who, in addition to her ordinary house duties, was busy in spinning and weaving the linen and woollen cloth needed for the family." He went to school at seven years of age, the school just then kept in a private house, as the schoolhouse was undergoing repair. His first teacher was one Joshua Coffin, afterwards author of a history of Newberry (not the teacher spoken of in " Snowbound "), an able though eccentric man, who, in various ways, was of service to the future poet. Usually there was but one school term in the year, lasting during three of the winter months. Little time or opportunity for much learning here, and but little chance of much home reading, with only about twenty volumes in the home library, the most of them journals and memoirs of the pioneers among the Friends. The much-read Bible was there of course. Other reading material consisted of the almanac and the weekly village newspaper. One book in the small library was the "Davideis," of Ellwood, the English Quaker and friend of Milton (to whom he read Greek, and who has the credit of having suggested "Paradise Regained"), a dreary poem of the Wars of King David; which might have helped young Whittier to a childish remark, that David could not have been a member of the Society of Friends, since he was so notable as a man of war.

Such questions will occur to the most piously brought up; and the boy Whittier missed no religious instruction. In that Quaker family Bible-reading was of course a constant practice, especially on First - day afternoons, when the mother read to the children, and sought to impress the meaning by familiar conversation—to which custom we may attribute the full and accurate knowledge of Bible history so conspicuous in Whittier's poems. On First - days the boy would sometimes be taken with the parents on their regular ride to the meeting-house at Amesbury; but, says the poet, "I think I rather enjoyed staying at home, wandering in the woods, or climbing Job's hill:" a smooth round grassy knoll in the neighbourhood, some three hundred feet high, from which is a beautiful view of the surrounding country. The woods hereabouts are very varied, oak, maple, walnut, fir, pine,—the colours of the foliage gorgeous in the late Indian summer. Surely, in

"The Barefoot Boy," he is recalling those early times
with good Uncle Moses !

> " Blessings on thee, little man !
> Barefoot boy, with cheek of tan,
> With thy turn'd-up pantaloons,
> And thy merry whistled tunes ;
> With thy red lip, redder still
> Kiss'd by strawberries on the hill ;
> With the sunshine on thy face
> Through thy torn brim's jaunty grace :
> From my heart I give thee joy,
> I was once a barefoot boy.
>
> .   .   .   .   .
>
> O for boyhood's painless play,
> Sleep that wakes in laughing day,
> Health that mocks the doctor's rules,
> Knowledge never learn'd in schools :
> Of the wild bee's morning chase,
> Of the wild flower's time and place,
> Flight of fowl and habitude
> Of the tenants of the wood ;
> How the tortoise bears his shell,
> How the woodchuck digs his cell,
> And the ground-mole sinks his well ;
> How the robin feeds her young,
> How the oriole's nest is hung ;
> Where the whitest lilies blow,
> Where the freshest berries grow,
> Where the ground-nut trails its vine,
> Where the wood-grape's clusters shine ;

Of the black wasp's cunning way,
Mason of his walls of clay,
And the architectural plans
Of grey hornet artisans !—
For, eschewing books and tasks,
Nature answers all he asks ;
Hand in hand with her he walks,
Face to face with her he talks,
Part and parcel of her joy :
Blessings on the barefoot boy !

O for boyhood's time of June,
Crowding years in one brief moon,
When all things I heard or saw
Me, their master, waited for !
I was rich in flowers and trees,
Humming-birds and honey-bees ;
For my sport the squirrel play'd,
Plied the snouted mole his spade ;
For my taste the blackberry cone
Purpled over hedge and stone ;
Laugh'd the brook for my delight,
Through the day and through the night
Whispering at the garden wall,
Talk'd with me from fall to fall ;
Mine the sand-rimm'd pickerel pond,
Mine the walnut slopes beyond,
Mine on bending orchard trees
Apples of Hesperides !
Still as my horizon grew
Larger grew my riches too ;

All the world I saw or knew
Seemed a complex Chinese toy,
Fashion'd for a barefoot boy.

O for festal dainties spread,
Like my bowl of milk and bread,
Pewter spoon and bowl of wood,
On the door-stone grey and rude !
O'er me, like a regal tent,
Cloudy-ribb'd the sunset bent,
Purple-curtain'd, fringed with gold,
Loop'd in many a wind-swung fold ;
While for music came the play
Of the pied frog's orchestra ;
And to light the noisy choir,
Lit the fly his lamp of fire.
I was monarch : pomp and joy
Waited on the barefoot boy."

So throve the child, the boy, on his pleasant path to manhood, under such good home influences, and with such happiest surroundings. Little was there of disturbance from the outside world. Tramps occasionally came, getting a kindlier treatment than now. "Twice a year," he tells us, "usually in the spring and autumn, we were honoured with a call from Jonathan Plummer, maker of verses, pedlar and poet, physician and parson, a Yankee troubadour—first and last minstrel of the valley of the Merrimac, encircled to my wondering young eyes with the very nimbus of immortality. He brought with him pins, needles, tape and cotton thread, for my mother; jack-knives, razors, and soap, for my father; and verses of his own composing, coarsely printed, and illustrated with rude woodcuts, for the delectation of the younger branches of the family. No love-sick youth could drown himself, no devoted maiden bewail the moon, no rogue mount the gallows, without fitting memorial in Plummer's verses. Earthquakes, fires, fevers, and shipwrecks, he regarded as personal favours from Providence, furnishing the raw material of song or ballad. Welcome to us in our country seclusion, as Autolycus to the clown in 'Winter's Tale,' we listened with infinite satisfaction to his reading of his own verses, or to his ready improvisation upon some domestic incident or topic suggested by his auditors. When once fairly over the difficulties at the outset of a new subject, his rhymes flowed freely, ' as if he had eaten ballads and all men's ears grew to his tunes.' His productions answered, as nearly as I can remember, to Shakspere's description of a proper ballad—'doleful matter merrily set down, or a very pleasant theme sung lamentably.' He was scrupulously conscientious, devout, inclined to theological disquisitions, and withal mighty in Scripture. He was thoroughly independent; flattered nobody, cared for nobody, trusted nobody. When invited to sit down at our dinner-table, he invariably took the precaution to place his basket of valuables between his legs for safe keeping. 'Never mind thy basket, Jonathan!' said my father; 'we sha'n't steal thy verses.' 'I'm not sure of that,' returned the suspicious guest. 'It is written, trust ye not in a brother!'"

" One day we had a call from a ' pawky auld carle ' of a wandering Scotchman. To him I owe my first introduction to the songs of Burns. After eating his bread and cheese, and drinking his mug of cider, he gave us ' Bonnie Doon,' ' Highland Mary,' and ' Auld Lang Syne.' He had a full rich voice, and entered heartily into the spirit of his lyrics. I have since listened to the same melodies ; but the skilful performance of the artist lacked the novel charm of the gaberlunzie's singing in the old farmhouse kitchen."

"When I was fourteen years old, my first schoolmaster, Joshua Coffin, brought with him to our house a volume of Burns' poems, from which he read, greatly to my delight. I begged him to leave the book with me, and set myself at once to the task of mastering the glossary of the Scottish dialect at its close. This was about the first poetry I had ever read, with the exception of that of the Bible (of which I had been a close student), and it had a lasting influence upon me. I began to make rhymes myself, and to imagine stories and adventures."

The attempts induced by reading Burns ("about the first poetry he had read," that of the " Davideis " perhaps not counted by him as such), were some little-noticeable imitations in dialect, not worthy of preservation. His earliest verse rather recalls the monotonous sing-song of Ellwood ; and he began to rhyme at a much earlier age than fourteen, as Mr. Kennedy reports, from an old friend and schoolmate in Haverhill, that Whittier, " instead of doing sums on his slate in school, was always writing verses even when a little lad." The native faculty needed no outer prompting, though the poetry of Burns would give an added impulse.

Whittier's first schooldays were when he was seven years of age, but the schooling was intermittent. As before said, there was but one term in the year, lasting three months of the winter, the boys being wanted at farm-work in the better weather. There was usually a new master every winter, and on the whole the facilities for education appear to have been very scanty. We have no information as to the amount, or intermittent amounts, of instruction which helped the mental growth of the boy poet. Some little book-knowledge may have been so obtained; but probably he learned more on the farm and in his holiday experiences with Uncle Moses. We get little more concerning him until 1826—he then 19—when William Lloyd Garrison, but three years his senior, had established in Newburyport the *Free Press*, for which the Whittier family subscribed, "pleased with the humanitarian tone of its articles." To this paper Whittier ventured to send a poem. It is not quite clear what this poem was, but it is taken to have been one (still in print) of thirty-one lines, in respectable but not remarkable blank verse, "The Deity," a fairly written amplification of the following passage in the 19th chapter of the First Book of Kings :—

"And behold the Lord passed by, and a great and strong wind rent the mountain and brake in pieces the rocks before the Lord, but the Lord was not in the wind; and after the wind an earthquake, but the Lord was not in the earthquake; and after the earthquake a fire, but the Lord was not in the fire; and after the fire a still small voice."

The poem, whether this or another, touched the heart of the editor, and was destined to have a most important influence on the life of the poet. We can imagine the pleasure of the author, still but a youth, at the first sight of his poem in the "Poet's Corner" of a newspaper,— his first appearance in print. He was at work with one of his elders mending fences when the news-carrier rode by, and, taking the paper from his saddle-bag, threw it to them. Whittier took it, saw his lines, read them of course on the spot, all work forgotten in the moment. It was the beginning of a poetic career.

One day, in the summer of 1826, he was hoeing in the field, when a carriage was driven to the house, and a visitor inquired for John Greenleaf Whittier. The youth hastened to the house in astonishment, entering by the back door, as he was not presentable in only shirt and trousers and straw hat. Who could have come to see *him?* It was the enthusiastic young editor of the *Free Press.*

The father called in, the son's prospects were discussed, the prudent father no doubt remonstrating against "putting notions in the boy's head," as Garrison expatiated on the capabilities which the early verses indicated, and urged the training needed by such talent at some public institution. But the farmer was not rich; the farm produce barely supplied the needs of the family, and there was no money. The lad himself met the difficulty. A young man who worked on the farm during the summer used the unemployed time in winter to make women's shoes; and offered to teach young Whittier. His offer was accepted, and during the following winter our poet learned the craft, and earned enough by his shoemaking to buy a suit of clothes and to pay for board and tuition tor six months at the academy in Haverhill.

CHAPTER VI.

IN April, 1827, in his twentieth year, Whittier went to the academy at Haverhill, a new building then occupied for the first time. There was a formal dedication, and the new scholar wrote the ode for the occasion. Here he pursued the ordinary English studies, and also had lessons in French. He remained there six months, during which time it was his custom to return every Friday evening to spend Saturday and Sunday at home. His ode, and the appearance in print, gave him distinction and a position in both the academy and the town.

He boarded with the family of Mr. Thayer, then editor and publisher of the *Haverhill Gazette.* Mrs. Thayer, still living in 1883, takes pleasure in recalling her impressions of the poet. She remembers his handsome face and figure, and the appearance of extreme neatness which he always bore; but she has more to say of the liveliness of his temper, his ready wit, his perfect courtesy, and infallible sense of truth and justice. On account of his abilities and exemplary conduct, no less than for his reputation as a rising poet, his society was much sought after. The gatherings of young people were never thought complete without

Whittier, and the young ladies of the school and village were never quite so happy as when from time to time invited to her house to tea. He was on a footing of intimacy with the Thayer family, their house his home whenever he was in Haverhill. Long after, when they went to Philadelphia, Mr. Thayer having set up a newspaper in that city, he became once more an inmate of their house.

Another Haverhill lady, Mrs. Harriet Pitman, a daughter of Judge Minot, writes of his appearance and character as seen by her at that time in her unmarried days : " He was a very handsome, distinguished-looking young man. His eyes were remarkably beautiful. He was tall, slight, and very erect, a bashful youth, but never awkward, my mother said, who was a better judge than I of such matters. He went to school at Haverhill Academy. There were pupils of all ages from ten to twenty-five. My brother George Minot, then about ten years old, used to say that Whittier was the best of all the big fellows, and he was in the habit of calling him Uncle Toby. He was always kind to children, and under a very grave and quiet exterior there was a real love of fun and a keen sense of the ludicrous. In society he was embarrassed, and his manners were in consequence sometimes brusque and cold. With intimate friends he talked a great deal and in a wonderfully interesting manner ; usually earnest, often analytical, and frequently playful. He had a great deal of wit ; it was a family characteristic. The study of human nature was very interesting to him, and his insight was keen. He liked to draw out his young friends, and to suggest puzzling doubts and queries. When a wrong was to be righted or an evil to be remedied, he was readier to act than any young man I ever knew, and was very wise in his action, shrewd, sensible, practical. The influence of his Quaker bringing-up was manifest. I think it was always his endeavour

> ' To render less
> The sum of human wretchedness.'

This, I say, was his stedfast endeavour, in spite of an inborn love of teasing. He was very modest, never conceited, never egotistic.

" One could never flatter him. I never tried ; but I have seen people attempt it, and it was a signal failure. He did not flatter, but told very wholesome and unpalatable truths, yet in a way to spare one's self-love by admitting a doubt whether he was in jest or earnest.

" The great questions of Calvinism were subjects of which he often talked in those early days. He was exceedingly conscientious. He cared for people, quite as much for the plainest and most uncultivated, if they were original and had something in them, as for the most polished.

" He was much interested in politics, and thoroughly posted. I remember, in one of his first calls at our house, being surprised at his conversation with my father upon Governor Gerry and the gerrymandering [1]

[1] Gerrymandering is the arbitrary and artificial dividing of a State into electoral districts in order to insure party elections. Pretty frequently practised, it would seem to owe its invention to this Governor Gerry.

of the State, or the attempt to do it, of which I had until then been ignorant.

"He had a retentive memory and a marvellous store of information on many subjects. I once saw a little commonplace book of his, full of quaint things and as interesting as Southey's.

"His house was one of the most delightful that I ever knew, situated in a green valley, where was a laughing brook, fine old trees, hills near by, and no end of wild-flowers. What did they want of the music and pictures which man makes when they had eyes to see the beauties of Nature, ears to hear its harmonies, and imaginations to reproduce them? It makes me impatient to hear people talk of the dulness and sordidness of young life in New England fifty years ago! There was Nature with its infinite variety; there were books, the best ever written, and not too many of them; there were young men and maidens with their eager enthusiasm; there were great problems to be solved, boundless fields of knowledge to explore, a heaven to believe in, and neighbours to do good to. Life was very full.

"Whittier's home was exceptionally charming on account of the character of its inmates. His father, a sensible and estimable man, died before I knew the home. His mother was serene, dignified, benevolent—a woman of good judgment, fond of reading the best books—a woman to honour and revere. His aunt, Mercy Hussey, who lived with them, was an incarnation of gracefulness and graciousness, of refinement and playfulness, an ideal lady. His sister Elizabeth, 'the youngest and the dearest,' shared his poetic gifts, and was a sweet rare person, devoted to her family and friends, kind to every one, full of love for all beautiful things, and so merry, when in good health, that her companionship was always exhilarating. I cannot imagine her doing a wrong thing or having an unworthy thought. She was deeply religious, and so were they all."

"I have said nothing of Whittier in his relations to women. There was never a particle of coxcombry about him. He was delicate and chivalrous, but paid few of the little attentions common in society. If a girl dropped her glove or handkerchief in his presence, she had to pick it up again, especially if she did it on purpose.

"I was about to speak of his thrift and frugality, and of his independence, and of his early taking upon himself the care of the family. . . . I have not mentioned the anti-slavery cause, the subject nearest to his heart after the year 1833, the subject about which he talked most, for which he laboured most, and to which he was most devoted. All his friends became Abolitionists. I was deeply in sympathy with him on this question ; but this is a matter of history, and he should recount his own experience."

Whittier wrote poems for the *Haverhill Gazette* (now out of print) as early as 1828, and perhaps earlier. At the close of his first term at the Academy, in the autumn of 1827, he had his one experience of teaching. During the winter he taught the district school at West Amesbury, now Merrimac. In the spring of 1828, he returned to the Academy at Haverhill for another six months' study.

Meantime, the *Free Press* failing, Garrison had gone to

Boston and started the *National Philanthropist*.   There, in the autumn of 1828, he found a place for Whittier as a writer (really editor, though not paid for editing) for the *American Manufacturer*, an advocate of protection to home industry.   His work on the paper was comparatively unimportant, and his salary, nine dollars a week, insufficient.   So his help being needed on the farm, he returned home in June, 1829, and there remained until July, 1830.   While at Boston he boarded for a short time in the same house with his friend Garrison.

From 1828 to 1830 he seems to have written much in both verse and prose ; nothing however very memorable. During the first six months of 1830 he edited, while still at home, the *Haverhill Gazette*, and wrote verse and prose for the *New England Review*, of Hartford, Connecticut.   Of the *Review*, in July, 1830, he became editor, and held that position for a year and a half.   Of over forty poems published during his editorship, he has cared to preserve but three in the complete editions of his works : those three—the " Frost Spirit," the " City of the Plain," and the " Vaudois Teacher,"—the last, many years ago translated into French, read and treasured among the primitive Protestants of the valleys of the Lower Alps ; for some time believed to be an original French poem.

For a time he lived in Hartford, but much of his work was done at home while there, on account of his father's failing health.   The father died in June, 1831, and Whittier went back to Hartford, reluctantly leaving his mother and sisters.   In the following January his want of health compelled him to give up the newspaper drudgery, his help also no doubt needed at the old homestead. He had previously, in February, 1831, published a small volume of "New England Legends," in prose and verse : a collection of stories, some in crude verse, beginnings of little worth and of not much promise. He had also edited the poems of his friend J. G. C. Brainard, a young man of amiable character, whose poetry, however, takes but an inconspicuous place in American anthology.

Of the early writing a good example is a brave apostrophe to New England, in the number for October, 1830, parts of which were afterwards incorporated in a longer poem, " Moll Pitcher, the Witch of Nahant," which has not been preserved. One passage from the *Review* may be worth quoting, as showing at least, the high thought which caused the poet's early endeavours.

> " Land of my fathers ! if the name,
>   Now humble and unwed to fame,
>   Hereafter burn upon the lip
>   As one of those which may not die,
>   Link'd in eternal fellowship
>   With visions pure and strong and high,—
>   If the wild dreams that quicken now
>   The throbbing pulse of heart and brow
>   Hereafter take a real form,
>   Like spectres changed to beings warm,
>   And over temples worn and grey
>   The starlike crown of glory shine,
>   Thine be the bard's undying lay,
>   The murmur of his praise be thine ! "

Now that the crown has rested upon the "temples worn and grey" we can well understand the devout feeling which inspired even that early verse. The same clear perceptions of the poet's mission, the mission indeed of every true and heroic man, is expressed more than forty years later in his lines on Sumner, prefaced by the following words from Milton's "Defence of the People of England": "I am not one who has disgraced beauty of sentiment by deformity of conduct, or the maxims of a freeman by the actions of a slave; but by the grace of God I have kept my life unsullied." These lines, the epitaph of the Massachusetts Senator, are as fitly applicable to himself, the young Abolitionist, on his setting forth in life.

> " God said,—Break thou these yokes! undo
> 　　These heavy burdens! I ordain
> 　A work to last thy whole life through,
> 　　A ministry of strife and pain.
>
> 　Forego thy dreams of letter'd ease;
> 　　Put thou the scholar's promise by!
> 　The rights of man are more than these.
> 　　He heard and answer'd—Here am I."

CHAPTER VII.

ON New Year's Day, 1831, Garrison sent forth his
first number of the *Liberator* from his attic at
No. 6, Merchant's Hall, Boston.   He had made a brief
attempt at Brattleborough in Vermont; had begun
again at Baltimore, and was there imprisoned for inability to pay fifty dollars, for damage and costs, at the
suit of a Massachusetts shipmaster, having libelled him
in calling him a pirate for shipping a cargo of slaves.
He was released after some weeks' incarceration on the
money being paid by Arthur Tappan, a wealthy merchant at one with the Abolitionists.   Then he tried
Washington, but finally decided on bringing out his
paper in Boston.   His only associate in the enterprise was
his friend Isaac Knapp, of Newburyport.   They, with a
negro boy to help, did the whole work, the editor himself
using the composing-stick.   The simple object of the
publication was what had to become a mere truism, but
then shocked the general reader as if it were a shriek of
terrific threatening : " *Unconditional emancipation is the
immediate duty of the master and the immediate right of
the slave* :" the purpose emphasised by the editor's
determination—" I will be as harsh as truth, as uncom-
promising as justice ; I am in earnest, I will not

equivocate, I will not excuse, I will not retreat a single inch, and I will be heard." So, as Luther stood when he had nailed his theses to the church door at Wittenburg, stood Garrison in Boston, beginning his apostleship, the suffering of derision, vilification, and violence,— civic officers, lawyers, and ministers of the gospel, vying in defamation and outrage, and having at last to accept the grand result of his toils and sufferings, and those of his friends and disciples, and to recognise him as of the noblest of the sons of Massachusetts.

On Whittier Garrison's influence was immediate. Heart and soul he was already with him. He too had gauged the iniquity of slave-holding, and recognised the call upon every earnest man to oppose it; and began his work with a considerable pamphlet, entitled " Justice and Expediency ; or, Slavery considered with a view to its rightful and effectual remedy, Abolition : " "an able and well-reasoned treatise, touching upon every point then in controversy, and fortified with abundant references to documents and statistics, covering the ground completely." It is so described by Mr. Underwood. Mr. Kennedy speaks of it as only a polemical paper, full of exclamation-points and italicised sentences. Yet he adds—" The pamphlet however shows diligent and systematic study of the entire literature of the subject. Every statement is fortified by quotation or reference."

The first edition of the pamphlet, printed at Haverhill in 1833, was at Whittier's own expense; but not long after, Louis Tappan, of New York, one of the early Abolitionists, brought out an edition of ten thousand for gratuitous distribution.

On the 4th of December, 1833, the Philadelphia Convention for the formation of the "American Anti-Slavery Society" held its first sitting, Beriah Green, president, Lewis Tappan and John G. Whittier, honorary secretaries. Lucretia Mott, a beautiful and graceful Quakeress—to be well known afterwards in the Abolitionist movement—was one of the speakers. "She offered," says Whittier, "some wise and valuable suggestions, in a clear, sweet voice, the charm of which I have never forgotten."

A committee, of which Whittier was a member and Garrison chairman, was appointed to draw up a Declaration of Principles. Garrison sat up all night to finish the drafting. When the other members of the committee rejoined him in the grey dawn of the December day, they found him still at work. His draft was accepted almost without amendment by the Convention, and signed by the sixty-two members present, twenty-one of whom were Quakers.

For the *Atlantic Monthly* for February, 1874, Whittier writes on this Convention, of his going and presence there. "In the grey twilight of a chill day of late November, forty years ago, a dear friend of mine residing in Boston made his appearance at the old farmhouse in East Haverhill. He had been deputed by the Abolitionists of the city, William L. Garrison, Samuel E. Sewall, and others, to inform me of my appointment as a delegate to the Convention to be held in Philadelphia for the formation of an American Anti-Slavery Society, and to urge upon me the necessity of my attendance.

"Few words of persuasion, however, were needed. I

was unused to travelling; my life had been spent on a secluded farm, and the journey, mostly by stage-coach, was really a formidable one. Moreover, the few Abolitionists were everywhere spoken against, their persons threatened, and in some instances a price set upon their heads by Southern legislatures. Pennsylvania was on the borders of slavery, and it needed small effort of imagination to picture to oneself the breaking up of the Convention and maltreatment of its members. This latter consideration I do not think weighed much with me, although I was better prepared for serious danger than for anything like personal indignity. I had read Governor Trumbull's description of the tarring and feathering of his hero MacFingal, when, after the application of the melted tar, the feather-bed was ripped open and shaken over him, until

> ' Not Maia's son with wings for ears
> Such plumes about his visage wears,
> Nor Milton's six-wing'd angel gathers
> Such superfluity of feathers,'

and I confess I was quite unwilling to undergo a martyrdom which my best friends could scarcely refrain from laughing at. But a summons like that of Garrison's bugle-blast could scarcely be unheeded by me who from birth and education held fast the traditions of that earlier Abolitionism which, under the lead of Benezet and Woolman, had effaced from the Society of Friends every vestige of slave-holding. I had thrown myself, with a young man's fervid enthusiasm, into a movement which commended itself to my reason and conscience, to my love of country and my sense of duty to God and my fellow-men. . . . I could not hesitate, but prepared at once for the journey. It was necessary that I should start on the morrow, and the intervening time, with a small allowance for sleep, was spent in providing for the care of the farm and homestead during my absence."

He writes further of those composing the Convention: —" Looking over the assembly, I noticed that it was mainly composed of comparatively young men ; some in middle age, and a few beyond that period. They were nearly all plainly dressed, with a view to comfort rather than elegance. Many of the faces turned toward me wore a look of expectancy and suppressed enthusiasm ; all had the earnestness which might be expected of men engaged in an enterprise beset with difficulty, and perhaps peril. The fine intellectual head of Garrison, prematurely bald, was conspicuous ; the sunny-faced young man at his side, in whom all the beatitudes seemed to find expression, was Samuel T. May, mingling in his veins the best blood of the Sewalls and Quincys ; a man so exceptionally pure and large-hearted, so genial, tender, and loving, that he could be faithful to truth and duty without making an enemy.

> ' The deil wad look into his face
> And swear he could na wrang him.'

That tall, gaunt, swarthy man, erect, eagle-faced, upon whose somewhat martial figure the Quaker coat seemed a little out of place, was Lindley Coates, known in all

Eastern Pennsylvania as a stern enemy of slavery; that slight, eager man, intensely alive in every feature and gesture, was Thomas Shipley, who for thirty years had been the protector of the free coloured people of Philadelphia, and whose name was whispered reverently in the slave-cabins of Maryland as the friend of the black man—one of a class peculiar to old Quakerism, who, in doing what they felt to be a duty and walking as the Light within guided them, knew no fear, and shrank from no sacrifice. Braver man the world has not known. Beside him, differing in creed, but united with him in works of love and charity, sat Thomas Whitson, of the Hicksite school of Friends, fresh from his farm in Lancaster County, dressed in plainest homespun, his tall form surmounted by a shock of unkempt hair, the odd obliquity of his vision contrasting strongly with the clearness and directness of his spiritual insight. Elizur Wright, the young professor of a Western college, who had lost his place by his bold advocacy of freedom, with a look of sharp concentration, in keeping with an intellect keen as a Damascus blade, closely watched the proceedings through his spectacles, opening his mouth only to speak directly to the purpose. . . . In front of me, awakening pleasant associations of the old homestead in Merrimac Valley, sat my first school-teacher Joshua Coffin, the learned and worthy antiquarian and historian of Newbury. A few spectators, mostly of the Hicksite division of Friends, were present in broadbrims and plain bonnets."

The year 1834 was passed by Whittier on the farm. In April of that year an anti-slavery society was formed at

Haverhill, of which he was corresponding secretary. The pro-slavery feeling, however, was as bitter there as elsewhere, shown forth on the occasion of the Rev. Samuel T. May attempting one Sabbath evening to give an anti-slavery lecture. In his " Recollections of the Anti-Slavery Conflict," we find the following account of the meeting held in the Free-Will Baptist Church—a large hall over a row of stores.

" I had spoken," said Mr. May, "about fifteen minutes, when the most hideous outcries, yells from a crowd of men who had surrounded the house, startled us; and then came heavy missiles against the doors and blinds of the windows. I persisted in speaking for a few minutes, hoping the blinds and doors were strong enough to stand the siege. But presently a heavy stone broke through one of the blinds, shattered a pane of glass, and fell upon the head of a lady sitting near the centre of the hall. She uttered a shriek, and fell bleeding into the arms of her sister. The panic-stricken audience rose *en masse*, and began a rush for the doors." Seeing the danger, Mr. May bade them pass out quietly and in order, as the platform outside was narrow and the stairs steep. He would stay to the last, and it was only against him that the crowd outside raged. He sent them safely out, he not going until the hall was nearly empty, when he went out, with Whittier's young sister on his arm, as she would not leave him. " Fortunately none of the ill-disposed knew me. So we passed through the lane of madmen unharmed, hearing their impreca-tions and threats of violence to the —— Abolitionist when he should come out."

Whittier was not present on this occasion. He was absent in New Hampshire, where he had the honour of a mob got up on his own account. George Thompson, the English Abolitionist lecturer, who about this time had been invited from England by Garrison, was especially obnoxious to the pro-slavery party. He narrowly escaped assault in Salem ; and for two weeks had to be secreted by Whittier at East Haverhill. Lecturing in Boston, an attempt was made to seize him and carry him to the South in a South Carolina vessel in wait for him. On the morning of the day appointed for the lecture to the Female Anti-Slavery Society, the following placard was posted in all parts of Boston :—

" THOMPSON THE ABOLITIONIST.

"That infamous foreign scoundrel, Thompson, will hold forth this afternoon at 46, Washington Street. The present is a fair opportunity for the friends of the Union to snake Thompson out. It will be a contest between the Abolitionists and the friends of the Union. A purse of *one hundred dollars* has been raised by a number of patriotic citizens to reward the individual who shall first lay violent hands on Thompson, so that he may be brought to the tar-kettle before dark. Friends of the Union ! be vigilant !"

At another meeting, in Boston, Garrison was laid hold of by a howling mob led by men of property and social standing, and, dragged through the streets with a rope round his neck, was only rescued by the police, who hurried him into Leverett Street Gaol as the only place of safety. How came our preacher-poet in such a crowd, he a Quaker, among other Quakers certainly, but perilling life by his daringly offensive speech ? Well might Lowell ask :—

" O leathern-clad Fox !
  Can that be thy son in the battle's mid din
  Preaching brotherly love, and then driving it in
  To the brain of the tough old Goliath of sin
  With the smoothest of pebbles from Castaly's spring
  Impressed on his hard moral sense with a sling ? "

Whittier himself, in some early writing, attempts to answer the question.

" Without intending any disparagement of my peaceable ancestry for many generations, I have still strong suspicions that somewhat of the old Norman blood, something of the grim Berserker spirit, has been bequeathed to me. How else can I account for the intense childish eagerness with which I listened to the stories of old campaigners who fought their battles over again in my hearing? Why did I, in my young fancy, go up with Jonathan, the son of Saul, to smite the garrisoned Philistines of Mickmash, or with the fierce son of Nun against the cities of Canaan? Why was Mr. Greatheart, in 'Pilgrim's Progress,' my favourite character? What gave such fascination to the narrative of the grand Homeric encounter between Christian and Apollyon in the valley? Why did I follow Ossian over Morven's battle-fields, exulting in the vulture-screams of the blind scald over his fallen enemies? . . . I can account for it only on the supposition that the mischief was inherited —an heirloom from the old sea-kings of the ninth century.

" Education and reflection have, indeed, since wrought a change in my feelings. . . . It is only when a great thought incarnates itself in action, desperately striving to

find utterance even in sabre-clash and gun-fire, or when
Truth and Freedom, in their mistaken zeal, and distrust-
ful of their own powers, put on battle-harness, that I can
feel any sympathy with merely physical daring. The
brawny butcher-work of men whose wits, like those of
Ajax, lie in their sinews, and who are 'yoked like
draught oxen, and made to plough up the wars,' is no
realisation of my ideal of true courage.

"Yet I am not conscious of having lost in any degree
my early admiration of heroic achievement. The feeling
remains, but it has found new and better objects. I have
learned to appreciate what Milton calls the martyr's
'unresistible might of meekness,' the calm, uncomplain-
ing endurance of those who can bear up against persecution uncheered by sympathy or applause, and, with a full
and keen appreciation of the value of all they are called
to sacrifice, confront danger and death in unselfish devotion to duty. Fox preaching through his prison gates or
rebuking Oliver Cromwell in the midst of his soldier
court; Harry Vane beneath the axe of the headsman;
Mary Dyer on the scaffold at Boston; Luther closing his
speech at Worms with the sublime emphasis of his 'Here
stand I, I cannot otherwise, God help me'; William
Penn defending the rights of Englishmen from the bale-
dock of the Fleet Prison; Clarkson climbing the decks
of Liverpool slave-ships; Howard penetrating to infested
dungeons; meek Sisters of Charity breathing contagion in
thronged hospitals,—all these, and such as these, now
help me to form the loftier ideal of Christian heroism.

" Blind Milton approaches nearly to my conception of
a true hero. What a picture have we of that sublime old

man as, sick, poor, blind, and abandoned of friends, he still held fast his heroic integrity, rebuking with his unbending republicanism the treachery, cowardice, and servility of his old associates! He had outlived the hopes and beatific visions of his youth; he had seen the loud-mouthed advocates of liberty throwing down a nation's freedom at the feet of the shameless, debauched, and perjured Charles II., crouching in the harlot-thronged court of the tyrant and forswearing at once their religion and their republicanism. The executioner's axe had been busy among his friends. Vane and Sidney slept in their bloody graves; Cromwell's ashes had been dragged from their resting-place; for even in death the effeminate monarch hated and feared the Conqueror of Naseby and Marston Moor. He was left alone in age and penury and blindness, oppressed with the knowledge that all which his fine soul abhorred had returned upon his beloved country. Yet the spirit of the stern old republican remained to the last unbroken, realising the truth of the language of his own 'Samson Agonistes':—

> ' But patience is more of the exercise
> Of saints, the trial of their fortitude,
> Making them each his own deliverer
> And victor over all
> That tyranny or fortune can inflict.'

"Who that has read his powerful appeal to his countrymen when they were on the eve of welcoming back the tyranny and misrule which at the expense of so much blood and treasure had been thrown off, can ever forget it? How nobly does Liberty speak through him!

'If,' said he, 'ye welcome back a monarchy, 'it will be the triumph of all tyrants hereafter over any people who shall resist oppression; and their song shall be to others, "How sped the rebellious English?" but to our posterity, "How sped the rebels, your fathers?"' How solemn and awful is his closing paragraph! 'What I have spoken is the language of that which is not called amiss the Good Old Cause. If it seem strange to say, it will not, I hope, seem more strange than convincing to backsliders. This much I should have said, though I were sure I should have spoken only to trees and stones, and had none to cry to but with the prophet, O earth! earth! earth! to tell the very soil itself what its perverse inhabitants are dead to; nay, though what I have spoken should prove (which Thou suffer not, who didst make mankind free, nor Thou next, who didst redeem us from being servants of sin!) to be the last words of our expiring liberties.'"

So lengthy a quotation may be allowed not merely for its eloquence, but as clearly exposing the motives which actuated our poet's conduct through life. The story of his public action is involved in the history of the Anti-Slavery movement.

CHAPTER VIII.

IT is a remarkable testimony to the esteem in which Whittier must have been held by his fellow citizens in Haverhill that, notwithstanding their bitter hatred of Abolitionism, they elected him as their representative to the State Legislature in 1835, and again in 1836. In 1837 he declined re-election. In the legislative documents for 1835 he appears as a member of the standing committee on engrossed bills. His name is not in the State records for 1836, doubtless owing to his inability to take his seat as a member of the Legislature, having been that year appointed Secretary to the American Anti-Slavery Society, which called him to Philadelphia.

" He was for many years an active politician," says the writer of his memoir in the New York *Nation*, "and esteemed a man of excellent judgment in all public matters. He was a keen judge of character, was perfectly unselfish, and always appeared to look at affairs more with the eyes of a man of the people than with those of a student. Without making any words about it, he seemed held by early association as well as principle to the point of view of the working class, . . . still nothing

to keep him from full identification with the most culti-
vated class."

In 1836 he published "Mogg Megone," a poem of
more than a thousand lines on an episode in Indian life,
the love of a chief for a white girl, and his death by her
hand. In 1837 he edited and prefaced the "Letters of
John Quincy Adams to his Constituents," and in the
same year edited "Views of Slavery and Emancipation,"
a pamphlet taken from Harriet Martineau's "Society in
America." During these years he also wrote a number of
occasional verses, published in 1838 by Joseph Knapp,
the publisher of the *Liberator*, as "Poems written during
the Progress of the Abolition Question in the United
States" between the years 1830 and 1838.

While in Philadelphia he edited the *Pennsylvania
Freeman*, the office of which and the Pennsylvanian Hall
(the hall of the Anti-Slavery Society in the same building)
were sacked and burned by a mob in May, 1838. The
hall had been built, at very considerable cost, in order
that there should be at least one place available for free
discussion. Of course that was reason enough for its
destruction. The keys had been given, and the protection of the building specially entrusted, to the Mayor of
Philadelphia, but neither he nor the police interfered
with the pro-slavery rioters.

A Southerner who witnessed, perhaps assisted at, the
fire, wrote an account of it for a New Orleans newspaper,
from which the following is taken, the italics our own :—

" At half-past seven p.m. the people, *feeling themselves
able and willing to do their duty*, burst open the doors of
the house, entered the Abolition book-store, and made

complete havoc of all within. They then beat out all the windows, and, gathering a pile of window-blinds and a pile of abolition books together, they placed them under the pulpit, and set fire to them and the building. . . . The multitude, as soon as they saw the building on fire, *gave a loud shout of joy.* A large number of splendid fire-engines were immediately on the spot, many of which could throw water more than a hundred feet high; but *the noble firemen,* to a man, of all the companies present, refused to throw one drop of water on the consuming building. All they did was to direct their engines to play upon the private buildings in the immediate vicinity of the blazing hall, some of which were in danger, as they were nearly joining the hall. . . . Such conduct in the Philadelphia fire-companies deserves the highest praise and gratitude of all friends of the Union, and of all Southerners in particular; and I hope and trust the fire-companies of New Orleans will hold a meeting and testify in some suitable manner to the Philadelphia fire-companies their *sincere approbation of their noble conduct* on this occasion."

Another Southerner writes to a Georgian paper how he and a friend helped, and enjoyed the spectacle. "We lent our feeble efforts to effect the demolition of this castle of iniquity. . . . The fire-companies repaired tardily to the scene of action, and not a drop of water did they pour upon that accursed Moloch until it was a heap of ruins. Sir! it would have gladdened your heart to have beheld that lofty tower of mischief enveloped in flames. The devouring element seemed to wear, combined with its terrible majesty, beauty and delight. To witness those beautiful spires of flame gave undoubted assurance to the heart of the Southron that in his brethren of the North he has friends who appreciate him, and who will defend him, though absent, at any and at every hazard."

Here we may fitly speak of the attitude of the main Quaker body with regard to the slavery question.

Through the exertions of John Woolman, Benjamin Lundy, Anthony Benezet, and others, the Friends had been brought to see the wickedness of slave-holding, and so early as 1784 had succeeded in ridding the denomination of the wrong. They not only freed their slaves, but also remunerated them for past service. Their record in this respect is unique for its devotion to exact and simple justice. They were the first religious sect as a body to have done with slavery. But the more worldly among them, prudent, acquisitive, ease-loving, were content to rest with having cleared their own skirts of the ill-doing. They could not see the necessity of the Abolitionists' movement for the conversion of others, and were fairly scandalised by the violence and fanaticism of some of the Abolitionist party. Whittier was grieved at this attitude of the society, but did not therefore break from it, nor abandon its distinctive religious views. In 1868 he wrote to the *New Bedford Standard*, which had misjudged him : "My object in referring to the article in the paper is mainly to correct a statement regarding myself, viz., that, in consequence of the opposition of the Society of Friends to the anti-slavery movement, I did not for years attend their meetings. This is not true. From my youth up, whenever my health permitted, I have been a constant attendant of our meetings for religious worship.

This is true, however, that, after our meeting-houses were denied by the yearly meeting for anti-slavery purposes, I did not feel it in my way, for some years, to attend the annual meeting at Newport. From a feeling of duty I protested against that decision when it was made, but was given to understand pretty distinctly that there was no 'weight' in my words. It was a hard day for reformers; some stifled their convictions; others, not adding patience to their faith, allowed themselves to be worried out of the society. Abolitionists holding office were very generally 'dropped out,' and the ark of the church staggered on with no profane anti-slavery hands upon it."

" After the sacking and burning of the office of the *Pennsylvania Freeman*, Whittier returned to Haverhill," —Mr. Kennedy's bare statement in such words implying an immediate departure; but, according to Mr. Underwood, the publication of the *Freeman* was with but little delay resumed (of course in other premises), and he remained in Philadelphia for somewhat more than a year, when, on account of failing health, he gave up the editorship and returned to Massachusetts.

In 1840 the old homestead at East Haverhill was sold; and the family, the mother, aunt, and younger sister, removed to Amesbury, partly for the sake of being near the Friends' meeting-house. The poet joined them there, making it his legal residence; although during the last few years of his life he spent much time at Oak Knoll, in Danvers, Massachusetts, the home of some attached relatives.

The four or five years, or more, following the removal

to Amesbury were filled with earnest work for the anti-slavery cause, done in straitened circumstances, for he had now to depend on his pen for his support. The time had not come for any great appreciation of his genius by the general public. It was sufficient to be an Abolitionist to put him outside the pale of literary sympathy. He wrote, however, constantly for the newspapers wherever he could obtain admission for his peculiar views; and he often went from town to town endeavouring to create anti-slavery sentiment, and to organise voters for effective service at the polls, sometimes lecturing, although not a ready orator, and, in his modest way, averse to speech-making. At this period his most intimate friend and fellow-labourer was Henry B. Stanton, afterwards of New York, and the two were great lobby-workers in the Massachusetts Legislature,—Whittier, strange as it may appear, according to Wendell Phillips, "a superb hand at it." With all the exterior calm of his Quaker quietude, he was a shrewd judge of men, and knew how to appeal to what was best in them. This steadily persistent work in politics, it need hardly be said never for other than moral ends, has never been neglected by him.

In 1844 he lived for six months in Lowell, writing for the *Middlesex Standard*, a Liberty paper. He was poorly paid, but it was congenial labour; indeed, he could not have written else. One series of papers in the *Standard* was afterwards reprinted in Boston, under the title of "The Stranger in Lowell." Some of these papers will be found in the second volume of his prose works.

The election of 1844 was the precursor of the Mexican

War, waged to extend the area of slavery, and thereby perpetuate its existence through Southern ascendency in the United States Government. To Whittier, opposed to both slavery and war, this appeared as an outrage— a crime against a people who had only too much reason for jealousy of the United States, a crime against humanity. His poems, written at this period, are remarkable for vigour and for their intensity of feeling. They appeared in many newspapers, and it would be difficult to assign exact dates to them ; their order in the collected editions being not chronological.

Here it may be well to glance briefly at the " Voices of Freedom " ("from 1833 to 1848 "), a volume published in 1849, by Lindsay and Blakeston, Philadelphia. Most of them were taken from files of the *Liberator*, *Emancipator*, *Anti-Slavery Standard*, *Haverhill Gazette*, and *National Era*. The contributions to the *Era* began in 1847, and reached a large number. The sources of these Voices, gathered from the newspapers for which they were originally written, are not given in the collection, and would be now found with difficulty, if at all.

We must remember, writes Mr. Underwood (whom we must follow in our chronicle of the poems, and whose own words we may therefore use as far as possible), that Whittier has regarded poetry as a means, and not an end. His aims had been (in all his early work) to reach the hearts of men, and poetic diction had been only the feathering of his arrows. Had he lived in a time when there were no oppressed to be set free, no wrongs to be redressed, no evils to be overthrown, he might have sung hymns

of pure beauty and joy, for no poet evinces a keener
sense of the divine in man, or a more ecstatic pleasure
in the divine manifestations in nature. Those who read
poems for intellectual pleasure will not feel attracted by
these strong utterances so much as by the legends,
ballads, and landscape pieces, farther on. But to the
elders, who were living in that dreary time, when evil
was good, injustice honoured, and God mocked, these
poems appear to embody all their thoughts, their labours,
their sufferings, and their aspirations. More than this,
they renew in the mind the glow with which they were
first read, as stanza succeeds stanza of impassioned
eloquence, paralleled only by the majestic burdens of the
prophets of old. One, entitled simply "Stanzas," from
the *Liberator*, of September, 1834, has an almost terrible
force.

"What, ho! *our* countrymen in chains!
  The whip on woman's shrinking flesh!
Our soil yet reddening with the stains
  Caught from her scourging, warm and fresh!
What! mothers from their children riven!
  What! God's own image bought and sold!
Americans to market driven,
  And barter'd as the brute, for gold!

Speak! shall their agony of prayer
  Come thrilling to our hearts in vain?
To us whose fathers scorn'd to bear
  The paltry menace of a chain;

To us whose boast is loud and long
  Of holy liberty and light :
Say ! shall these writhing slaves of Wrong
  Plead vainly for their plunder'd Right ?

. . . . .

Shall every flap of England's flag
  Proclaim that all around are free
From farthest Ind to each blue crag
  That beetles o'er the Western Sea:
And shall we scoff at Europe's kings
  When Freedom's fire is dim with us ;
And round our country's altar clings
  The damning shade of Slavery's curse ?

. . . . .

Up, then, in Freedom's manly part,
  From grey-beard old to fiery youth,
And on the nation's naked heart
  Scatter the living coals of Truth !
Up !—while ye slumber, deeper yet
  The shadow of our fame is growing ;
Up !—while ye pause our sun may set
  In blood around our altars flowing."

Evidently written in a white heat, the language is at
once terse and vehement, and the sound of the lines is
like the clashing of swords.

Perhaps the most brilliant and most aggressive of these
poems is the one entitled " The Pastoral Letter," first
printed in the *Liberator*, in October, 1837.   A council of
Congregational clergymen, at Brookfield, Massachusetts,
had taken occasion to discourage the agitation of the

question of slavery, and they censured especially the employment of female anti-slavery speakers, quoting Paul, after the old fashion. This was directed mainly against the accomplished sisters, Sarah and Angelina Grimké, Carolina's high-souled daughters," who had been slave-owners, and who now as advocates of freedom were making trouble for the quietist preachers by awakening the consciences of their hearers. The reply of Whittier is filled with grim sarcasm and indignant invective. The blood of his Quaker ancestors was in a ferment. The lines hit like rapier-thrusts. The memory of clerical oppression, and of the wrongs inflicted upon his people in Puritan times would not be restrained.

   .   .   .   .   .   .

"A ' Pastoral Letter,' grave and dull !
    Alas ! in hoof and horns and features,
  How different is your Brookfield bull
    From him who bellows from St. Peter's.
Your pastoral rights and powers from harm,
    Think ye, can words alone preserve them ?
  Your wiser fathers taught the arm
    And sword of temporal power to serve them.

O glorious days, when Church and State
    Were wedded by your spiritual fathers,
And on submissive shoulders sate
    Your Wilsons and your Cotton Mathers !
No ' vile itinerant ' then could mar
    The beauty of your tranquil Zion,
But at the peril of the scar
    Of hangman's whip and branding-iron.

Then wholesome laws relieved the Church
  Of heretic and mischief maker ;
And priest and bailiff join'd in search,
  By turns, of Papist, Witch, and Quaker.
The stocks were at each church's door,
  The gallows stood on Boston Common ;
A Papist's ears the pillory bore,
  The gallows-rope a Quaker woman.

Your fathers dealt not as ye deal
  With ' non-professing ' frantic teachers ;
They bored the tongue with red-hot steel,
  And flay'd the backs of ' female preachers.'
Old Newbury, had her fields a tongue,
  And Salem's streets could tell their story
Of fainting women dragg'd along,
  Gash'd by the whip, accursed and gory.

And will ye ask me why this taunt
  Of memories sacred from the scorner,
And why with restless hand I plant
  A nettle on the graves ye honour ?
Not to reproach New England's dead
  This record from the past I summon,
Of manhood to the scaffold led,
  And suffering and heroic woman.

No !—for yourselves alone I turn
  The pages of intolerance over,
That in their spirit dark and stern
  Ye haply may your own discover.
.   .   .   .   .   .

And what are ye who strive with God
    Against the ark of His salvation,
Moved by the breath of prayer abroad
    With blessings for a dying nation ?
What but the stubble and the hay
    To perish, even as flax consuming,
With all that bars His glorious way,
    Before the brightness of His coming."

As a piece of literary workmanship (if such a phrase can be used in reference to an evident impromptu) this is not surpassed by any of the author's poems. So Mr. Underwood. It is indeed a very noticeable impromptu, coming in white heat from the heart, without care or need of studied rhymes or measures. Truly this Quaker had not his Berserker blood for nothing, nor read his Burns to no purpose.

The stated meetings of the anti-slavery societies were almost always enlivened and warmed by some new poem from Whittier, as well as by the magnificent oratory of Wendell Phillips. Many of the " Voices " were first uttered on these occasions, as their titles indicate. The reader will find them uniformly strong, religious, hopeful. The following, " Written for the Celebration of the Third Anniversary of British Emancipation," at the Broadway Tabernacle, New York, August 1, 1837, may be sample of the religious, hymn-like feeling, not always ungentle, which characterised so many of them. Indeed, many have been appropriated in collections of Hymns.

" O, Holy Father ! just and true
    Are all Thy works and words and ways,

And unto Thee alone are due
  Thanksgiving and eternal praise.
As children of Thy gracious care,
  We veil the eye, we bend the knee;
With broken words of praise and prayer,
  Father and God! we come to Thee.

For Thou hast heard, O God of Right!
  The sighing of the Island slave,
And stretch'd for him the arm of might,
  Not shorten'd that it could not save.
The labourer sits beneath his vine;
  The shackled soul and hand are free:
Thanksgiving! for the work is Thine;
  Praise! for the blessing is of Thee.

  .   .   .   .   .   .

Speed on thy work, Lord God of Hosts!
  And when the bondman's chain is riven,
And swells from all our guilty coasts
  The anthem of the free to heaven,
O, not to those whom thou hast led
  As with thy cloud and fire before,
But unto Thee in fear and dread
  Be praise and glory evermore!"

If (still borrowing from Mr. Underwood), if the conservative is still unable to appreciate the merits of the "Voices," the anti-slavery man, who bore his part in the long and often desperate conflict, is perhaps equally disqualified to form an impartial opinion. In his mind and memory the "Voices" are associated with all his toils and his triumphs; they represent his inmost feelings at the time when they were profoundly moved. They accord with his deepest convictions of right and duty; and their high solemn phrases seem to come with a divine authority. For an Abolitionist to assume a critical attitude in regard to the "Voices," would be as hard as for a Hebrew to find fault with "The Horse and his Rider," or "By the Waters of Babylon." It will be for neither of the parties that were engaged in the long and momentous struggle to decide upon the purely poetical merit of these lyrics. If the prime test of poetry were to be its power to move the heart, there could be but one opinion; but we must remember that impassioned eloquence, which is not necessarily poetical, does the same thing. There are many of Whittier's ringing stanzas which are scarcely more than rhymed eloquence; but, judged by the same rule, some of the most stirring passages of Byron and Dryden, and nearly all the heroic verses of Pope, come into the same category.

One more observation. In certain of the most outspoken of the "Voices," such as the "Pine Tree," "Massachusetts to Virginia," "Texas," and the "Branded Hand," there seems to prevail a spirit which is not only intense, but fierce. But those who understand the reality of the danger then impending, which was the entire subjection of the Government to the Slave Power, will not only pardon but applaud the energy with which the momentous issue was met. It was felt by all far-seeing men to be a question of life and death; and in such a terrible crisis courtesy would have been folly, and compliment crime. It was a combat *à outrance*.

Here is part of the fiercest and most declamatory,—who now will say " uncalled for," " too fierce," " too fervently violent in its prompting "—the " Pine Tree," written in 1846.

> " Lift again the stately emblem
>   on the Bay State's rusted shield !
> Give to Northern winds the Pine Tree
>   on our banner's tatter'd field !
> Sons of men who sat in council
>   with their Bibles round the board,
> Answering England's royal missive
>   with a firm ' *Thus saith the Lord !* '
> Rise again for home and freedom !
>   set the battle in array !
> What the fathers did of old time,
>   we their sons must do to-day.
>
> Tell us not of banks and tariffs !
>   cease your paltry pedlar cries !
> Shall the good State sink her honour
>   that your gambling stocks may rise ?
> Would ye barter men for cotton ;
>   that your gains may sum up higher,
> Must we kiss the feet of Moloch,
>   pass our children through the fire ?
> Is the dollar only real,
>   God and Truth and Right a dream ?
> Weigh'd against your lying ledgers,
>   must our manhood kick the beam ?

O my God ! for that free spirit
  which of old in Boston town
Smote the Province House with terror,
  struck the crest of Andros down ;
For another strong-voiced Adams
  in the City's streets to cry
Up for God and Massachusetts !
  set your feet on Mammon's lie !
Perish banks and perish traffic,
  spin you cotton's latest pound,
But in heaven's name keep your honour !
  Keep the heart o' the Bay State sound !"

We cannot desire that even one of the "Voices"
should have been silenced, uttered as they were at the
stern call of duty. The "burden" was upon the poet
as upon the old Hebrew prophet. And what is the
poet if not a seer ? Whose but his the prophetic
mission ? Whittier never faltered in his mission. His
part in the great revolution is now historical ; and after
its triumphant success, he could look back with more
than satisfaction upon the results he had aided in
bringing about.

CHAPTER IX.

W E can now look upon what, to a certain extent,
may be called his purely literary work, partially
beginning, indeed, so early as 1832.   Either in Hartford,
or shortly after his return to Haverhill, he wrote a long
poem called "Moll Pitcher," already mentioned.   Some
passages had appeared in his newspaper, but in the completed poem the main portions were new.   Moll Pitcher
was a fortune-teller, famous in the last century ; and the
story is of a country maiden and her sailor lover.   The
poem, writes the author in a prefatory note, "was
written during a few weeks of such leisure as is afforded
by indisposition, and is given to the world in all its
original negligence."   So little he thought of it that it
never was reprinted.   The short quotation, given by
Mr. Underwood, would show it to be in the measure
and manner of Scott's poems, only not so good.   Concerning it, the *New England Magazine* reviewer, May,
1832, while admiring certain portions for their versifica-
tion, is not very complimentary.   This magazine had
made its first appearance in 1831, under the editorship
of Joseph T. Buckingham, continuing to December,

1835, nine volumes, when it was merged in the *American Monthly Magazine* of New York. To Buckingham Lowell's first series of the "Biglow Papers" was addressed. John O. Sargent, a noted journalist of the time, and Dr. S. G. Howe, the educator of the blind, succeeded Mr. Buckingham, at the beginning of the eighth volume, but soon gave up the editorship to Park Benjamin, a writer of both prose and verse, a brother-in-law of the historian Motley.

The writers for the magazine, having no compensation but the publicity of their writing, were not always of the highest class. Many of the papers read like themes of undergraduates, or moral essays by budding clergymen. But there was a leaven in the midst. About a dozen of Wendell Holmes' humorous, yet tender and graceful early poems appeared during the first two years. Whittier furnished four prose writings and seven short poems. There were also poems by Mrs. Sigourney, James G. Percival, and other minors; and Hawthorne's "Twice-told Tales" made here their first appearance. The magazine was poorly printed upon dingy paper, and was "illustrated" with bad lithographs, only interesting for their subjects, not as works of art.

Whittier's contributions consist of "Powow Hill," a prose sketch, 1832; "Passaconaway," a prose story, 1833; the "Opium-Eater," prose, 1833; the "Female Martyr," a poem, 1833; "Stanzas," "Toussaint L'Ouverture," "A Lament," "Suicide Pond," the "Demon of the Study" (humorous), "Lines to Governor McDuffie," and "Mogg Megone"—these all poems.

During these years also occur the earlier poems of

the "Voices of Freedom," which form a group by themselves.

His writings in the *Democratic Review*, during a period of nine years are, in 1837, "Palestine"; in 1838, the "Familists' Hymn" and "Pentucket"; in 1841, "Democracy"; in 1842, "Follen," "Capital Punishment," and "Raphael"; in 1843, "To the Reformers of England," "Cassandra Southwick," "The Human Sacrifice," "Hampton Beach," "The New Wife and the Old," and a prose sketch of "James Naylor"; in 1844, "Channing" and "Ezekiel"; in 1844–6, "The Bridal of Pennacook," "Ronge," and "Songs of Labour."

Also, appearing in 1843, was a series of papers, "The Supernaturalism of New England," published as a volume in New York; reprinted in London in 1847.

To trace all Whittier's poems to their original publication is impossible. There was a collection of those on anti-slavery in a volume entitled the *North Star*, published in Philadelphia. The "Prisoner for Debt" appeared in an annual called the *Boston Pearl;* the "Fountain" in the *New York Mirror;* "To Massachusetts" in the *Emancipator;* a large number of the "Voices" and others in the *Liberator;* and many of the earliest in the *Haverhill Gazette*, as already noted. A considerable number still remain concerning which nothing of their first appearance is yet discovered. A small, now scarce, collection in 1843, "Lays of my Home and other Poems," with a dedication to John Pierpont, the preacher and poet, was published by W. D. Ticknor. It contained the "Merrimac," the "Norsemen," "Cassandra Southwick," "Funeral Tree of the

Sokokis," "Lines written in the Book of a Friend," " Lucy Hooper," " Follen," "To a Friend on her return from Europe," " Raphael," " Democracy," "Capital Punishment," the " Cypress Tree of Ceylon," " Chalkley Hall," "To the Reformers of England," " Massachusetts to Virginia," " Leggett's Monument," "To —— with Woolman's Journal," " Memories," the "Demon of the Study," the " Relic," " Extract from a New England Legend."

During the years from 1833 to 1848 the "Voices of Freedom " continued to appear, though after a time not only as lyrics, but sometimes lengthening out to the ballad form. Such are the " Branded Hand," " St. John " (a Huguenot legend), the " Exile," the " Old Wife and the New," and " Cassandra Southwick," which last is a perfect ballad.

It is a story of 1658, of a young Quaker girl sentenced in Boston, for her religion, to be transported to Virginia, and there sold as a slave. She is brought from prison to where the merchant ships are at anchor, and the shipmen are asked who will take charge of her.

> " But grey heads shook and young brows knit
>   the while the sheriff read
> That law the wicked rulers
>   against the poor have made.
>
> .   .   .   .
>
> Grim and silent stood the captains,
>   and when again he cried,
> 'Speak out, my worthy seamen !'
>   no voice, no sign replied ;

But I felt a hard hand press my own,
   and kind words met my ear :
'God bless thee, and preserve thee,
   my gentle girl and dear ! '

A weight seem'd lifted from my heart,
   a pitying friend was nigh ;
I felt it in his hard rough hand,
   and saw it in his eye ;
And when again the Sheriff spoke,
   that voice so kind to me
Growl'd back its stormy answer,
   like the roaring of the sea.

'Pile my ship with bars of silver,
   pack with coins of Spanish gold
From keel-piece up to deck-plank
   the roomage of her hold,
By the living God who made me,
   I would sooner in your bay
Sink ship and crew and cargo
   than bear this child away ! '

' Well answer'd, worthy captain !
   shame on their cruel laws ! '
Ran through the crowd in murmurs loud
   the people's just applause.
' Like the herdsman of Tekoa,
   in Israel of old,
Shall we see the poor and righteous
   again for silver sold ? '

I look'd on haughty Endicott
   with weapon half-way drawn,
Swept round the throng his lion glare
   of bitter hate and scorn ;
Fiercely he drew his bridle-rein
   and turn'd in silence back,
And sneering priest and baffled clerk
   rode murmuring in his track.

Hard after them the Sheriff look'd,
   in bitterness of soul ;
Thrice smote his staff upon the ground,
   and crush'd his parchment roll.
' Good friends ! ' he said, ' since both have fled,
   the ruler and the priest,
Judge ye, if from their farther work
   I be not well released.'

Loud was the cheer which full and clear
   swept round the silent bay,
As with kind words and kinder looks,
   he bade me go my way :
For He who turns the courses
   of the streamlet of the glen
And the river of great waters,
   had turn'd the hearts of men."

They who have pondered over the letters and journals
of Quakers under bonds and stripes, and in exile, will
feel how perfectly in this brave ballad Whittier has
reproduced the simple heroic trust in God which sustained so many martyrs. Of a very different character

is the tenderly beautiful lyric, " Memories," from which
also some stanzas must be quoted.

   .   .   .   .   .

" How thrills once more the lengthening chain
    Of memory at the thought of thee !
Old hopes which long in dust have lain,
Old dreams come thronging back again,
    And boyhood lives again in me :
I feel its glow upon my cheek,
    Its fulness of the heart is mine,
As when I lean'd to hear thee speak,
    Or raised my doubtful eye to thine.

I hear again thy low replies,
    I feel thy arm within my own,
And timidly again uprise
The fringèd lids of hazel eyes
    With soft brown tresses overblown.
Ah ! memories of sweet summer eves,
    Of moonlit wave and willowy way,
Of stars and flowers and dewy leaves,
    And smiles and tones more dear than they !

Ere this thy quiet eye hath smiled
    My picture of thy youth to see,
When, half a woman, half a child,
Thy very artlessness beguiled,
    And folly's self seem'd wise in thee.
I, too, can smile when o'er that hour
    The lights of memory backward stream,

    Yet feel the while that manhood's power
      Is vainer than my boyhood's dream.

        .   .   .   .

    Yet hath thy spirit left on me
      An impress time hath worn not out;
    A something of myself in thee,
    A shadow from the past, I see
      Lingering even yet thy way about.
    Not wholly can the heart unlearn
      That lesson of its better hours,
    Nor yet has Time's dull footstep worn
      To common dust that path of flowers."

There is no record of any such story concerning our poet; but these lines seem to suggest an early love, perhaps a disappointment accounting for his not having married. We have a glimpse to the same purport in a much later poem, the "Dream of the Sea," in "My Playmate," and also in the following extract from a prose essay, "My Summer with Dr. Singletary" :—

" 'It is long since I have looked at my old school-day companions, the classics,' said Elder Staples ; 'but I remember Horace only as a light, witty, careless Epicurean, famous for his lyrics in praise of Falernian wine and questionable women.'

" 'Somewhat too much of that, doubtless,' said the Doctor, 'but to me Horace is serious and profoundly suggestive, nevertheless. Had I lain him aside on quitting college, as you did, I should perhaps have only remembered such of his Epicurean lyrics as recom-

mended themselves to the warm fancy of boyhood.
Ah, Elder Staples! there was a time when the Lyces
and Glyceras of the poet were no fiction to us. They
played blindman's-buff with us in the farmer's kitchen,
sang with us in the meeting-house, and romped and
laughed with us at huskings and quilting parties. Grand-
mothers and sober spinsters as they now are, the change
in us is perhaps greater than in them.'

"'Too true!' replied the Elder, the smile which had
just played over his pale face fading into something
sadder than its habitual melancholy; 'the living companions of our youth whom we daily meet are more
strange to us than the dead in yonder graveyard. *They*
alone remain unchanged.'"

In that early edition of 1843 the Merrimac River
appears in many poems of its scenery and historic associations: in the "Bridal of Ponnacook," the "Laurels,"
"Sewall's Prophecy," the "Exiles," "Pentucket," the
Swan Song of Parson Avery," and others. Burns and
Scott have made Scottish streams and mountains classic;
but no poet has more fully identified himself with the
beauty of Nature in the region of his birth than
Whittier. And the Merrimac is a worthy subject for
song. It receives the flow of springs and the melting
of mountain snows in the middle district of New Hampshire, including the overflow from its chief lake, Winne-
pesauke, and from the streams of the Pemigewasset
Valley; it traverses the deep grassy meadows near
Concord, studded with native elms; it is for a time
troubled in the rapids of Suncook and Hookset until

it comes in view of the rounded loveliness of the twin Unacanoonucs ("woman's breasts" in the Indian tongue), and then dashes down the wild rocky cascades of Amoskeag, where now are the factory-piles of Manchester. From this its course is through scenes of tranquil beauty, in green meadows and under trees, until its successive falls at Nashua, Lowell, and Lawrence, turning laborious wheels ; whence it flows without hindrance, except for an occasional island, past Haverhill and Amesbury, to reach the sea at Ipswich Bay, between Newburyport and Salisbury.

Geologists term it a mountain trough ; and at the outset, before the current becomes polluted by the dyes and refuse of mills, the water is pure crystal. Above Lowell the water-bed is narrow, and the banks are but little raised, although elevations of sand and gravel on either side often testify to the force of the waters in remote periods. But below the last falls the river-bed is wider and the banks stretch out on either hand. The tourist, whether he follows the road on the northern or southern side, will find himself on a high ridge, with a wide valley between him and the actual river-bank ; and, looking across the river, will see that the whole basin is frequently more than a mile in width.

The unusual breadth of the valley is due to the action of glaciers, moving seaward, blocking the waters and grinding their way. The whole of the lower part of the river-bed and valley, from Pentucket Falls, is full of the wreckage of the ancient rocks torn from their beds during the glacial period. But Nature has been repairing the ravages and covering the abraded surfaces of the hills with trees and soft turfy coats, forming the *roches moutonnées*, as the hills rounded in the glacial period are termed.

The regions personally known to Whittier, those particularly referred to in his verse, include the eastenr portions of Massachusetts and Rhode Island, the south-eastern part of New Hampshire, and the coast of Maine. We can see that his feet have overgone the lands he describes. Two poems in the edition of 1843 show that the knowledge of Maine was already gained. In one, the ballad of "St. John," he recalls the strife, for mastery of the coast, between the Protestants under La Tour and the Catholics under d'Aulney, French nobles, whose names are frequently to be met with in the Colonial records. This ballad gives a striking picture of the early time when exiled Huguenot and Royalist strove for existence. Strangely as the writing of a Quaker (but the Berserker fire was not all gone out), its phrases ring as if the maker had heard the clang of steel. In the "Funeral Tree of the Sokokis" the local colouring is true and strong. The scenery of the Saco, even now grand and impressive despite the ravages of lumber-men, is restored in the poet's verse to its primitive loneliness.

It will be seen that Whittier did not confine his sympathies to the African slaves, nor even to the persecuted of his own Quaker sect; his generous spirit embraced the whole of suffering humanity. The wrongs of the Indians were often a theme for him ; he sympathised with the republican hopes of Europe in 1848 ; the prisoner for debt shared his pity ; and with all his energy he protested against death-punishment.   These traits are continually exhibited.   The anti-slavery poems in the edition of 1843 are few, not out of proportion to the rest.   It was a book for the unprejudiced to read. But the time for general appreciation had not come.

CHAPTER X.

THE *National Era* was established at Washington in 1847, and became one of the leading organs of the anti-slavery party. Its editor, Dr. Gamaliel Bailey, a man of literary predilections and culture, was wise enough to secure the aid of good writers. Whittier was engaged as assistant or corresponding editor, and the connection lasted until the end of 1857. "Uncle Tom's Cabin" appeared as a serial in the *Era* in 1850. The sisters Alice and Phœbe Cary, and Lucy Larcom, contributed poems; and bright and witty prose came from the pens of "Grace Greenwood" and "Gail Hamilton." Whittier wrote more than eighty poems for it (from 1847 to 1859), in power, variety, and interest exceeding any series, except perhaps what he afterward gave to the *Atlantic Monthly*. Some of them—though in that time the poet's sustained and more artistic power steadily grew—are hardly surpassed by his later productions. In the first number appeared "Randolph of Roanoke," one of the finest of his political poems, and full of generous feeling. Others were "Maud Muller" (so well known), the "Burial of Barbour," "The Witch's Daughter," "Tauler," "Barclay of Ury," and "Ichabod." "Barclay of Ury," though one of his best ballads, contains the Quaker impress. Its hero was among the earliest converts in Scotland to the doctrines of the Friends. Though an old soldier of Protestantism who had fought with distinction under Gustavus Adolphus in the German war, he, when he became a Quaker, was the object of persecution and abuse at the hands of the magistracy and the populace. How the proud gentleman and soldier bore the indignities of the mob is well related in the ballad :—

> "Up the streets of Aberdeen,
>   By the kirk and college-green,
>   Rode the Laird of Ury ;
>   Close behind him, close beside,
>   Foul of mouth and evil-eyed,
>   Press'd the mob in fury.
>
>   Flouted him the drunken churl,
>   Jeer'd at him the serving-girl,
>   Prompt to please her master ;
>   And the begging carlin, late
>   Fed and clothed at Ury's gate,
>   Cursed him as he pass'd her.
>
>   Yet with calm and stately mien
>   Up the streets of Aberdeen
>   Came he, slowly riding ;
>   And to all he saw and heard
>   Answering not with bitter word,
>   Turning not for chiding.

Came a troop with broadswords swinging,
Bits and bridles sharply ringing,
   Loose and free and forward;
Quoth the foremost, 'Ride him down!
Push him! prick him! through the town
   Drive the Quaker coward!'

But from out the thickening crowd
Cried a sudden voice and loud—
   'Barclay! ho, a Barclay!'
And the old man at his side
Saw a comrade, battle-tried,
   Scarr'd and sunburnt darkly,

Who with ready weapon bare,
Fronting to the troopers there,
   Cried aloud—'God save us!
Call ye coward him who stood
Ankle-deep in Lutzen's blood
   With the brave Gustavus?'

'Nay! I do not need thy sword,
Comrade mine!' said Ury's lord;
   'Put it up! I pray thee.
Passive to His holy will,
Trust I in my Master still,
   Even though He slay me.

'Pledges of thy love and faith,
Proved on many a field of death,
   Not by me are needed.'

Marvel'd much that henchman bold
That his lord, so stout of old,
   Now so meekly pleaded.

'Woe's the day!' he sadly said,
With a slowly shaking head,
   And a look of pity;
'Ury's honest lord reviled,
Mock of knave, and sport of child,
   In his own good city.

'Speak the word, and, Master mine!
As we charged on Tilly's line
   And his Walloon lancers,
Smiting through their midst we'll teach
Civil look and decent speech
   To these boyish prancers.'

'Marvel not, mine ancient friend!
Like beginning, like the end,'
   Quoth the Laird of Ury:
'Is the sinful servant more
Than his gracious Lord who bore
   Bonds and stripes in Jewry?

'Give me joy that in His name
I can bear with patient frame
   All these vain ones offer!
While for them He suffereth long,
Shall I answer wrong with wrong,
   Scoffing with the scoffer?

' Happier I, with loss of all,
Hunted, outlaw'd, held in thrall,
  With few friends to greet me,
Than when reeve and squire were seen
Riding out from Aberdeen
  With bared heads to meet me.

' When each good wife, o'er and o'er,
Bless'd me as I pass'd her door ;
  And the snooded daughter,
Through her casement glancing down,
Smiled on him who bore renown
  From red fields of slaughter.

' Hard to feel the stranger's scoff,
Hard the old friend's falling off,
  Hard to learn forgiving :
But the Lord His own rewards,
And His love with theirs accords,
  Warm, and fresh, and living.

' Through this dark and stormy night
Faith beholds a feeble light
  Up the blackness streaking ;
Knowing God's own time is best,
In a patient hope I rest
  For the full day-breaking.'

So the Laird of Ury said,
Turning slow his horse's head
  Tow'rd the Tolbooth prison,

Where through iron gates he heard
Poor disciples of the Word
Preach of Christ arisen."

Four more stanzas, not necessary to its completion,
conclude the ballad. Not infrequently, the poet lacks
the artistic instinct that would stay his impulsive pen.
Always good, we still could sometimes spare the moral.
Of "Ichabod" we need every word : the stern but not
unpitying rebuke of Webster for a compromising speech
which permitted the passing of the Fugitive Slave Bill,
that crowning insult to the Free States of the Union.

"So fallen ! so lost ! the light withdrawn
Which once he wore !
The glory from his grey hairs gone
For evermore !

Revile him not ! the tempter hath
A snare for all ;
And pitying tears, not scorn and wrath,
Befit his fall.

O, dumb be passion's stormy rage,
When he who might
Have lighted up and led his age
Falls back in night !

Scorn ! would the angels laugh to mark
A bright soul driven,
Fiend-goaded, down the endless dark,
From hope and heaven ?

Let not the land once proud of him
   Insult him now,
Nor brand with deeper shame his dim
   Dishonour'd brow !

But let its humbled sons, instead,
   From sea to lake,
A long lament, as for the dead,
   In sadness make !

Of all we loved and honour'd nought
   Save power remains,
A fallen angel's pride of thought
   Still strong in chains.

All else is gone ; from those great eyes
   The soul has fled :
When faith is lost, when honour dies,
   The man is dead.

Then pay the reverence of old days
   To his dead fame !
Walk backward, with averted gaze,
   And hide the shame ! "

It is not mere rhetoric, but poetry, powerful and perfect in structure, reminding us of Browning's "Lost Leader," but simpler, stronger than that : the indignant yet dignified utterance of a proud regret for one who had been admired and loved ; sad, for what is sadder than the loss of faith in one of the high gods of our idolatry ?

Though we may perceive and note the progression of the poet, the reader should bear in mind that the political and purely artistic works of Whittier cannot be separated into periods. He always had many irons in the fire. His contributions to the magazines and other periodicals were parallel with his devoted labours for the anti-slavery cause, and his poems as well as his prose articles were widely distributed. The *Liberator*, the *Emancipator*, and the *Anti-Slavery Standard* contain original poems written during the same period as those in the *Era ;* and, as he and his seem to have been considered common property, his poems frequently appear in more than one paper, without acknowledgment, so rendering it doubtful for which they were written. From the time he began to write for the *Era*, however, his contributions were less scattered, and the other anti-slavery papers generally acknowledged the borrowing. For several years, indeed, he wrote almost exclusively for that paper, until the establishment of the *Atlantic Monthly* in 1857, after which a larger number of his poems went to that magazine.

Numerous as are his poems in the *Era*, the bulk of his work was in prose. A series of biographical sketches, entitled " Old Portraits," and a number of the papers in a series of " Literary Recreations," appeared first in the *Era*. Here, too, beyond question his most able and fortunate prose work, " Margaret Smith's Journal," first saw the light. This was reprinted in 1849, by Ticknor, Reed, and Fields ; and forms part, with the " Portraits " and " Recreations " of a two-volume edition of " Prose Works," published by Ticknor and Fields, in 1866.

Of these prose works, the "Portraits," if not adding to his fame on purely literary grounds, though they are well written, are yet interesting to the biographer as showing the men in whom he took such special interest, and so are worth naming—John Bunyan; Thomas Ellwood, who read to Milton in his days of blindness, and suggested to him the writing of "Paradise Regained;" poor enthusiastic, sometimes mad, James Naylor; Andrew Marvell; John Roberts, the Cromwellian soldier, and afterwards Quaker-farmer (a review of "Memoirs of John Roberts, *alias* Haywood, by his son Daniel," a pleasant old narrative, to be found in only a few Quaker libraries); Samuel Hopkins, of Connecticut, ultra-Calvinist, also one of the first to plainly denounce the slave-trade and slavery of the Africans; brave Richard Baxter, who held personal controversy with Cromwell himself; William Leggett, a true man and true democrat, of whom Whittier writes: "What Fletcher of Saltoun is to Scotland and the brave spirits of the old Commonwealth time,

> 'The later Sidney, Marvell, Harrington,
>   Young Vane, and others who call'd Milton friend,'

are to England, should Leggett be to America:" Nathaniel Peabody Rogers, with "much in character and genius to remind us of the gentle author of 'Elia'"; and Robert Dinsmore, Irish born, with Scotch forbears, who in America served in the Revolutionary army, and who was the imitative Burns in the village newspaper of Haverhill in Whittier's young days. These show our poet's leanings, not at any time narrowed to his own

sect, however closely his religious opinions held him to
that.

Of the "Literary Recreations" he himself speaks
slightingly. "Penned at widely different periods in
every variety of mood and circumstance, . . . their
selection from a large amount of similar matter destined
in all human probability to that capacious wallet

> 'Which Time hath ever at his back,
>   Wherein he puts alms to oblivion,'

has been owing quite as much to the fact that they lay
nearest at hand as to any estimate of their relative fitness
or merit; . . . they were written at times when any
more serious effort would have been irksome and painful,
and they afforded the necessary episodical relief of an
intense and over-earnest life. A publisher's volume
indeed, and so for the author's sake to be leniently
judged." There are thirty-five of these papers, of which
a few, not perhaps the most important, may be named to
show their character—"Utopian Schemes and Political
Theorists," "Peculiar Institutions of Massachusetts,"
"Carlyle on the Slave Question," "England under
James II." (a review of Macaulay's History), "The
Border Wars of 1708," "The Black Men in the Revolution" (a vindication of their services then), "My Summer
with Dr. Singletary," "The Little Iron Soldier," "Pentucket Falls," "Yankee Gypsies," "The Scottish Reformers." Of these "My Summer with Dr. Singletary"
is the most considerable, and of greater length than any
of the rest: a pleasant gossipy descriptive essay in six
chapters. But all the thirty-five papers will be read

with interest, and are not unworthy of being collected and preserved.

"Margaret Smith's Journal" is a more noteworthy book, belonging to the class of which examples are to be found in "The Household of Sir Thomas More," "The Maiden and Married Life of Mary Powell, afterwards Mistress Milton," and "The Artist's Married Life, being that of Albert Dürer." Strictly speaking, it is an historical novel, though to the modern novel-reader it will perhaps seem hardly a novel at all, but only a dry series of sketches of character, manners, and scenery, done in antique phraseology. To any one who has a smack of the tastes of an antiquary there can scarcely be a more delightful book. It is not oppressively learned or archaic; the fair young English girl who is supposed to chronicle her sojourn among her American relatives at Boston, and on the Merrimac and elsewhere in Yankeeland, from May, 1678, to November, 1679, is not a Quaker nor other sectary, but sincerely of the Church of England, so that the view is from without, free from prejudice and uncircumscribed. There is a slender thread of story, continuous enough to give a sense of real life ; and the style, perfect for its purpose, is far less rigid and crabbed than the usual writings of the time. Secretary Rawson, Sir Christopher Gardiner, Judge Samuel Sewall, Robert Pike, Richard Saltonstall, Rev. Mr. Ward, the "simple Cobbler of Agawam," Eliot the Apostle, Cotton Mather, Simon Bradstreet, and other personages seen by turns in the narrative, are drawn by a capable hand. Their conversation is separately, vitally characteristic, and every detail is in such perfect keeping that the *vrai-semblance* grows upon the reader, and time and place become present. There is no parallel to this book in the prose literature of the United States. For full enjoyment, indeed, of the book may require that the reader must own a kindred taste for a chastened view of life and for the beauty to be seen in humble and familiar things. It should be added that the religious questions in which the colonists at the supposed time of the journal were so deeply interested, are treated with honest candour, and yet with generosity and an almost touching delicacy. Margaret herself cannot have much sympathy with the exalted feeling and strained demeanour of some she met, who, according to the point from which they might be regarded, were fanatics or martyrs ; but she manifests a sweet courtesy, not to say pity, for those who incurred ecclesiastical and secular penalties for following the dictates of conscience.

Many poems and scraps of verse are interspersed, some of them in imitation of the laboured and pedantic style of the Rev. Michael Wigglesworth and Mrs. Ann Bradstreet of early colonial fame. Two, " Autumn Thoughts " and the ballad of " Kathleen," appear again in the " Complete Poems."

It is such a book as might have been written by Leigh Hunt, or rather by Lamb. They would have been delighted with it. Unowned, it might have been taken for the dainty work of the authoress of " Cranford," or have passed as the veritable journal of a true English girl of the time. One could fancy, if the date would suit, that Elizabeth Whittier, whose few graceful poems are not undeservedly printed with the complete Whittier, might have helped her brother with it.

CHAPTER XI.

THERE was a collection of Whittier's poems made in 1849, published by B. B. Mussey and Co., in a large and handsome octavo volume, with illustrations in steel by H. Billings. Mr. Mussey was a prominent Free-soiler, had presided at a State Convention of the party, and took pride in the reputation of the Poet of Freedom. It was the first time that Whittier's verse had been considered likely to be profitable as a speculation, even with the aid of pictorial illustration. Mussey dying in 1855, the plates were purchased by Ticknor and Fields. This Mussey edition contained a few poems which have since been dropped out; but the bulk remains in the standard edition, unchanged. It may, however, be observed that in regard to historical and topographical notes the Mussey edition was more satisfactory. The full significance and justification of the earlier verse must be lost to the modern reader; and even as to later events it should be remembered that the beginning of the anti-slavery struggle is behind the recollection of the present generation, and it will not be long before all of the younger poet's work, and how much of his maturity, all indeed that may be classed as political or occasional, will need annotation.

Of the "Songs of Labour," four were published in 1845–6, in the *Democratic Review*—the "Ship-Builders," the "Shoemakers," the "Fishermen," and the "Lumbermen." The "Drovers," the "Huskers," the "Corn-Song," and the "Dedication" were written later for the *National Era*. And the series was issued as a volume by Ticknor and Fields, in 1850. These are bright and cheery poems, in accord with the cheerful and energetic character of the thriving New England artizans of their period. The verse is good common-sense, one may say common-place, of the table-land of poetry on which Charles Mackay earned his popularity, but far below the heights of Parnassus. We may spare room for a characteristic stanza from the "Shoemakers."

> " Thy songs, Hans Sachs ! are living yet
>   In strong and hearty German ;
> And Bloomfield's lay, and Gifford's wit,
>   And patriot fame of Sherman ;
> Still from his book, a mystic seer,
>   The soul of Behmen teaches,
> And England's priestcraft shakes to hear
>   Of Fox's leathern breeches."

In 1852 a selection of his poems was published in London by Routledge. In 1853 was published the "Chapel of the Hermits," reprinted from the *Era*. In 1854 appeared in book-form the last, not last written, of his prose works, "Literary Recreations." In 1857 came the "complete" edition of Ticknor and Fields, to be supplemented by later completion in after years.

In this year 1857 Whittier's mother died, aged 77. She had lived to see the fruition of her hopes in his widespread fame as a poet and in the appreciation of his noble character as a man. The elder sister, Mary, married to Mr. Caldwell, lived to 1861 ; and the younger, Elizabeth, until 1864. Uncle Moses had died in 1824. The poet's only brother, Matthew, was alive until the 7th of January, 1883. Matthew seems to have been not without some talent, a maker of verses, and a contributor to newspapers of humorous dialect articles, over the signature of " Ethan Spike, from Hornby."

The life of Whittier from the time he had his home at Amesbury was uneventful. As before said, he lived six months at Lowell in the year 1845, but there was no other change in his quiet course. He had become known to widening circles of readers, and he found employment for his pen ; but there were no epochs except the publications of successive volumes. It may be a fair opportunity here to note some poems, written after the issue of the volume of 1843, that need comment as referring to persons or events. Whittier has seldom taken any pains to give explanation of scenes or portraits, both probably considered sufficiently obvious to the readers on the first appearance. But time passes, and later readers lose for want of explanatory words. The poem of the " Hero," written for the *National Era*, is a case in point. New Englanders, and others acquainted with the public men and institutions of Boston, would have no difficulty in deciding who he was, after seeing that the Hero had served as a soldier in the Greek war for independence, had been imprisoned in Germany, and afterwards had become an instructor and helper of the blind and dumb, and foremost in philanthropic movements; but few to-day in the West, or especially in England, would recognise the portrait as that of Dr. Samuel G. Howe, the husband of Julia Ward Howe, the authoress of that most stirring of the lyrics of the American War, the "Battle Hymn of the Republic" :—

> "Mine eyes have seen the glory of the coming of the Lord;
>   He is trampling out the vintage where the grapes of wrath are
>   stored;
>   He hath loosed the fateful lightning of His terrible swift sword;
>   His truth is marching on."

Many who, even personally, were acquainted with Dr. Howe, might not have known, till Whittier told them, of the earlier heroism of the good physician and teacher of the afflicted in Boston, the man

> "Who might wear the crest of Bayard
>   Or Sidney's plume of snow.
>
>   .   .   .   .   .   .
>
>   Once, when o'er purple mountains
>   Died away the Grecian sun,
>   And the far Cyllenian ranges
>   Paled and darken'd one by one,—
>
>
>   Fell the Turk, a bolt of thunder
>   Cleaving all the quiet sky,
>   And against his sharp steel lightnings
>   Stood the Suliote but to die.

Woe for the weak and halting !
   The crescent blazed behind,
A curving line of sabres,
   Like fire before the wind.

Last to fly, and first to rally,
   Rode he of whom I speak,
When, groaning in his bridle-path
   Sank down a wounded Greek.

   .   .   .   .   .   .

He look'd forward to the mountains,
   Back on foes that never spare,
Then flung him from his saddle
   And placed the stranger there.

' Allah ! hu !' Through flashing sabres,
   Through a stormy hail of lead,
The good Thessalian charger
   Up the slopes of olive sped.

Hot spurr'd the turban'd riders ;
   He almost felt their breath
Where mountain stream roll'd darkly down
   Between the hills and death.

One brave and manful struggle,—
   He gain'd the solid land
And the cover of the mountains
   And the carbines of his band.

' It was very great and noble,'
   Said the moist-eyed listener then ;
' But one brave deed makes no hero ;
   Tell what he since hath been ! '

.   .   .   .   .

Wouldst know him now?   Behold him
   The Cadmus of the blind,
Giving the dumb lip language,
   The idiot clay a mind !

.   .   .   .   .   .

Said I not well that Bayards
   And Sidneys still are here ? "

Well could our stern, fierce-voiced Abolitionist sing the
praise of the hero, showing how his own scornful hate
of Wrong grew fairly from his love and full appreciation
of the beauty of the Right.   May we not, when most
critically censorious, forgive him for some remainder of
Berserker fury, stirring in fearful need the saintly gentle-
ness of his soul ?

And who in foreign lands, or even of American birth,
except only some of our eldest, can now feel all the
significance of the tribute to "Rantoul" (*Era*, 1853)—
Robert Rantoul, the young senator from Massachusetts,
Webster's successor, who had thoughts of liberty for all
men, not liberty for only white men, a man able and
accomplished, on whom the hopes of the free-soilers
were laid, hopes dashed by his sudden death?

Turning now to "Calef in Boston" (*Era*, 1849), which
of us knows who was Calef?   Every one has read of the
terrible witch-time in Massachusetts, and most persons

may know how the Rev. Cotton Mather was the leading
spirit in those trials, ministering to the popular supersti-
tions by as credulous accounts of demoniac possession,
and spurring on judges to exterminate the wretches on
whom suspicion fell. His book, "Wonders of the Invisible World Displayed," is well known to all students
of the early colonial annals. But the general reader is
less likely to know that Robert Calef, a Boston merchant,
wrote in 1700 a common-sense reply, entitled, " More
Wonders of the Invisible World," which had a powerful
influence in quelling the excitement against witchcraft.
This book was very naturally denounced by the bewitched
clergy, and had the honour of being publicly burned in
the yard of Harvard College, by order of the president,
Increase Mather. The Mathers and their antagonist
lie peacefully together in Copp's Hill burying-ground in
the north end of Boston.

The occasion for the " Branded Hand " has been
already noted. The hand was that of Captain Jonathan
Walker, a ship-master of Harwich, Massachusetts. The
appeals to "Faneuil Hall " and to " Massachusetts "
were written on the near approach of the war against
Mexico; and the "Pine Tree," in a still more passionate
strain, called on the public to unite against the schemes
for the extension of slavery which followed that war.
Remembering that the first *national* anti-slavery party
was formed at Buffalo, in 1848, under the leadership of
Van Buren and Adams, we shall understand the "Pæan."
Lines to " a Southern Statesman " were addressed to John
C. Calhoun. "Leggett's Monument " is a tribute to an
intrepid man, once the associate of Bryant in his editorial

labours, whose monument was built by those who had contemned and resisted his efforts in the cause of freedom.

Eulogistic, but never adulatory, are many of Whittier's poems, but the eulogy has not been for the world's heroes and favourites. He has given his tributes of sympathy and affection rather to those whom the world despised or neglected. "Barclay of Ury" is an example of this championship of the unpopular. He has praiseful words for William Forster (the worthy Quaker father of our English statesman); for Daniel Wheeler (a Quaker preacher who laboured for his Divine Master in Great Britain, Russia, and the islands of the Pacific); for Daniel Neall ("friend of the slave and yet the friend of all"); for Channing and his fellow Abolitionists, Storrs and Torrey. It may fairly be said that his praise was never undeserved. The same also is to be said of his personal censures, even of the most severe, "Ichabod." It is worthy of remark that, at a public breakfast given in 1877 in honour of Whittier, Emerson chose this very poem to read as his tribute of admiration for the poet.

To connect the anti-slavery poems of this period (before 1860) it is necessary to bear in mind the history of the time. The Fugitive Slave Law was enacted in 1850 as part of the compromise consented to by Webster, and though the number of persons returned to slavery was small, the enforcement of the law was carried out in an odious manner, with the design of humiliating the North. From this came occasions for the poems "Moloch in State Street" (Boston), the "Rendition," the

"Voices," "Stanzas for the Times" ("The evil days have come"), "A Sabbath Scene," and others.

Very soon came the struggle between Northern and Southern emigrants for the possession of Kansas and Nebraska, and Fremont's candidature for the Presidency. Though in this sharp competition Fremont was unsuccessful, the North won, and the friends of freedom were cheered on by some of Whittier's most spirited lyrics, "To Pennsylvania," the "Pass of the Sierra," the "Kansas Emigrants," the "New Exodus," &c. The freedom of these new States was not established without bloodshed, as guerillas from Missouri made continual raids upon the "Yankee" settlements, butchering men and women by scores. One of these massacres in 1858 is the subject of "Le Marais du Cygne" (The Swan's Marsh). The "Burial of Barbour" (one of the Northern emigrants) had a like suggestion.

One simple and straightforward poem, wholly without angry alloy, good verse, if not marked by the highest poetical qualities, is "Our State," a hearty tribute to the worth of his native Massachusetts, for all her slavish shortcomings. Lines "to A. K." (*Era*, 1850) were to Avis Keene, a woman-preacher of the Society of Friends, referred to also in "The Meeting":—

> "Whose eighty years but added grace
> And saintlier meaning to her face,
> The look of one who bore away
> Glad tidings from the hills of day,
> While all our hearts went forth to meet
> The coming of her beautiful feet."

" Mary Garvin " (*Era*, 1856) tells of the return home of a grandchild whose mother had been carried off to Canada and there become a Catholic,—a not unlikely happening in days when the region of conflict and romance was in Canada and Northern Woods. In Chase's "History of Haverhill" there is preserved a letter of one Mary Wainwright, whose daughter had been captured by the French or French-siding Indians, in which she petitions the Governor and Council and Assembly of Massachusetts for her recovery, "that some care may be taken for her redemption before Canada is so endeared to her that I shall never have my daughter more."

The lake in "Summer by the Lakeside" is Lake Winnipiseogee, or, as it is now more commonly spelled, Winnepesaukee, situated in central New Hampshire, where it receives the brooks and melted snows of the White Mountains. Another, more important, of the poems of this period is the "Last Walk in Autumn" (1856–7), one of those perfect landscape pictures in the delineation of which the Whittier of these his maturer times stands unrivalled.

One more poem of the period, "My Namesake," addressed to Francis Greenleaf Allinson, of Burlington, New Jersey, deserves a special notice for its curious, quaint, truth-telling lines, which read as almost autobiographical. It is too long to be quoted in its entirety, and a few of its many stanzas would not give a fair idea of it.

To return to the "Voices of Freedom," the lyrics or the ballads of the battle-time, the cries of warning or encouragement,—what other conflict for human rights was ever accompanied by such fervent appeals to conscience, honour, and valour? Bryant, Longfellow, and Emerson gave timely aid with words, and the weight of their names, to the cause of freedom; Lowell, employing all the resources of wit and sarcasm, made the heads of the North keep time to his Yankee lyrics, and touched their hearts with more solemn song; but Whittier appeared to live for no other purpose than to sound the strenuous summons to duty at each occasion, his life a bugle-call, a call to be heard and to be obeyed. Yet more for their music than the words the "Marseillaise," and the "Chant du Départ" stand lyrically alone in that great time of trial in France, and no crisis so severe has called out the poets of England since the Commonwealth. The poetry of the anti-slavery movement in America exceeds in mere bulk, as it does in inspiration, power, and beauty, in its close application to passing events, all the poems written directly on subjects of great national importance in these latter centuries. Shelley's "Masque of Anarchy" is the one striking exception. Change of ministers or of dynasties, wars foreign or domestic, tariffs, franchises, landtenures, could hardly inspire so lofty thoughts or lead to such exaltation of feeling as have characterised the poets, *the* poet especially, and the orators of this anti-slavery era. It is notable, too, that natures perhaps far from poetic in grain became fired with the general enthusiasm and broke out in song. The universal air was aflame. Garrison himself at times wrote noble lines; Pierpont's heart beat audibly; and Theodore Parker and Wendell Phillips made every audience to thrill with the spirit that moves the solid world.

We look back as through smoke and flame to that eventful period, and we cannot but be grateful to have lived when great thoughts, eternal principles, and sublime ideals actuated men. From these days of most important traffic back to those when men were ready to peril and to devote life for the faith that was in them—can it be that it is but a quarter of a century, and not half a century since the worn heart of Europe also throbbed high with enthusiasm and hopes of the Republic?

In 1857, when the complete edition of poems already written was published by Ticknor and Fields, Whittier, then in his fiftieth year, had reached a position of universally recognised eminence. He had become famous by the natural development and exhibition of his faculties, carried on the wave of an incoming tide of popular interest in the question which chiefly occupied him, and without aid of friendly reviews or political or social influences. Like Garrison, he *would* be heard. Simply, unpretentiously independent, he used no arts to gain popular favour, nor sought in any way for homage. He was distinctly eminent as a man, and admired not solely as a poet. He was now invited to take part in the organisation of the *Atlantic Monthly*, and cordially gave the aid of his work and name. An attempt to combine the power of the leading writers of the North in behalf of the cause to which his life was devoted, could not be other than a matter of moment to him. To such importance had the cause of the abolition of slavery arisen by the persistent labour of himself, and the earnest despised friends among whom he had won renown.

Whatever other agencies had been employed, it is

but fair to say that the *Atlantic Monthly* was the first periodical of high rank in which the best literary work, poetry, fiction, essays, and criticism were all gathered in one sheaf in aid of the great moral question of the day. To such opportunity for successful propagandism had the times grown up from when Garrison and Knapp were found " working in an obscure hole, with a negro for sole assistant." The publishers, Phillips, Sampson and Co., had handsome quarters in Winter Street, Boston, and the meeting there of Abolitionists, Whittier, Lowell, Emerson, Parker, with the more purely literary contributors, Longfellow, Holmes, Prescott, Motley, Norton, Cabot, and Trowbridge, made the house a centre of attraction. The pay of the writers was liberal for the times, and this, together with the prestige which from the first attended the enterprise, drew sufficient contributions from every part of the Union, and from England.

The *Atlantic Monthly* took hold, and as it was the only literary periodical in America which discussed moral and political questions with freedom, it undoubtedly gave tone and direction to public thought. The name of Abolitionist came to be less opprobious, even to have a certain distinction. The little group which supported the magazine fortunately comprised not only the highest literary names, but names of men of standing in society. It was a time, too, of a breaking up of political parties, and men's minds were so more open to independent influences. Forced discussion, passionate appeal, such as had been successfully employed in the anti-slavery journals, and necessarily so in breaking ground, would have swamped the later magazine, or destroyed its influence with the classes to be reached. So the contributors were agreed to leave questions of politics to the editor. Whittier's poems for the first three years were upon general subjects, with the single exception of " Le Marais du Cygne," provoked by a massacre by pro-slavery ruffians in Kansas. Even then he seems to have paid unwonted deference to outside judgment. He writes, May 4, 1858 :—

" My dear friend, I am heartily obliged to thee for thy kind suggestions. But see what has been the result of them ! Is the piece better or worse ? Who knows ? My sister thinks she does, and that I have altered for the better. I hope it will strike thee and Lowell in the same way. The sweep and rhythm please me, but I have had hard work to keep down my indignation. I feel a good deal more like a wild Bersark than like a carpet minstrel with his singing robes about him when recording atrocities like that of ' The Swan's Marsh.' "

He had at last begun to care for the purely artistic side of his poetry, true artist at the core, though as a true man, when the humanitarian purpose was of immediate consequence, he could not be content with the pleasure of verbal and rhythmical perfection. In his " Skipper Ireson's Ride " the refrain was first written without the old Marblehead dialect. His attention was called to this, and he adopted the old-time phraseology :—

> " Here's Fludd Oirson, fur his horrd hoort,
> Torr'd an' futherr'd an' corrd in a corrt
> By the women o' Marble'ead."

Making the alteration, he returned the poem with the

gracious acknowledgment: " I thank thee for sending the proof with thy suggestions. I adopt them, as thou wilt see, mainly. It is an improvement. As it stands now, I like the thing well—'hugely,' as Captain Shandy would say."

There was a breathing time before the War. In 1860 appeared a volume of " Home Ballads, Poems, and Lyrics," prefaced by a dedicatory poem to some unnamed friend of the poet's youth. The chief place in the book was given to the " Witch's Daughter," a poem afterwards to appear, somewhat lengthened, renamed " Mabel Martin," as an illustrated holiday book. The story, said to be substantially true, is founded on a tradition in the neighbourhood of Amesbury, where the house of Mabel's father was still in existence not many years ago. The poem is one of the most charming of Whittier's ballads, set fitly in a landscape background, full of masterly touches, and breathing throughout a noble and humane spirit.

The " Prophecy of Samuel Sewall " is rich in historic allusion and a fine manliness. The " Sycamores " were trees planted on the highway, opposite to the Saltonstall Mansion, a short distance from Haverhill; but a few of them now remaining. The poem "To G. B. C." is a tribute to a celebrated preacher and editor, the Rev. George B. Cheever. The " Preacher " is Whitefield, the famous revivalist, who after his labours in Georgia, came to Massachusetts, and finished his work in Newburyport, where he was buried beneath the church that bears his name. " Telling the Bees " refers to a New England prevalent custom, brought from the old country.

On the death of a member of a family, the bees were at once informed of it, and their hives were draped in mourning. This was supposed to be necessary to prevent the bees from leaving their hives to seek a new home. This most perfectly beautiful idyll will need particular notice when we come to consider and sum up the characteristics of Whittier's poetry.

In the " Peace of Europe," the " Prisoners of Naples," and " From Perugia " (a grim record of the pontifical massacre there), we see the deep interest he took in the republican uprisings in the Europe of 1848. Not on the religious ground (he a man most tolerant in religion) were his feelings stirred against the Papacy ; but the fiery heat in which these utterances were cast was excited by his human sympathy for the victims of a cruel despotism. When Pope Pius IX. became the accomplice of Bomba of Naples and the " Crowned Scandal " Louis Napoleon,—that " barnacle on the dead renown of his uncle,"—aiding them to put down the hopes of liberty-loving men raised momentarily by success, and to inflict the bloody and remorseless punishments that everywhere followed, the Head of the Church could not shelter himself under any ecclesiastical subterfuge. He and Cardinal Antonelli were as distinctly responsible for the retributions in the Papal States as was Napoleon III. for the massacre of the *Coup d'Etat* which inaugurated his empire.

CHAPTER XII.

THE date of John Brown's attempt to incite an insurrection of the Southern slaves is 1859. Brown belonged to a plain Massachusetts family, which traced its descent from one of the Pilgrims of the *Mayflower*. He was a simple, hard-working, God-fearing man, abhorring slavery and war; and in less stirring times would probably have lived and died on a farm in New England or Ohio, known only as a self-reliant, just, and blameless citizen. But he had established for himself a lonely home on the borders of the Aidorondack region, and long meditating there on the radical injustice of slavery, his mind took a fixed direction, and everything with him became secondary to the one purpose for which he learned to live. This purpose grew to dominate all his actions, so that it might, by calmer men, be called insanity. But it was far from the insanity of the "insane." It was but the over-tension of a noble singleness of heart such as animated George Fox or Gordon, a singleness of heart and will that would not hesitate even at throwing himself away. And the time was eventful. The admission of Kansas as a State was under consideration. Was it to be a Slave State, to reinforce the South, or could it be kept free ? Northern men, attempting to settle in Kansas, were murdered by bands of pro-slavery guerillas from Missouri. A relentless warfare went on. Brown went down there, to settle on the side of freedom. He and his four sons were in these frays, and on several occasions by his intrepidity and masterly conduct he inflicted terrible loss on bodies of men far more numerous than those he could bring together. Once, with only thirty men, at Ossawatomie, he held at bay a force of five hundred until he made a retreat in safety. This gave him the name of Ossawatomie Brown. His doings during these years toward making the soil free in Kanas would fill a volume.

A deeper scheme was in his mind. He had become interested in many escaped slaves, who were naturally the most courageous of their class ; and he conceived the idea of arming the coloured people of the South and leading them to the establishment of their freedom. For this end he visited Boston and other places in New England, and sought to raise money. His real aim he kept to himself; those who aided him with money supposed that they were contributing for the defence of the Free-soilers in Kansas.

" In person " (this from one who had known him) " Brown was below the middle height, lean and sinewy. His long hair, nearly grey, was combed back in a smooth mass, leaving clear a high forehead, and below it a pair of wonderful grey eyes. His manner had a singular deliberation, under which the surging of a fiery soul was apparent. He related some of his exploits, and calmly told of the retribution that had fallen upon the slayers of two of his sons. In describing the pitiful massacres he had witnessed, and the death of his sons, and the sufferings of his sons' families, his voice never faltered, no tears dimmed his steady eyes. There was an inward fire, however, of which his measured words gave no sign. He·was a remarkable man, with every trait that goes to make up a hero, except for the lack of sound judgment." The after judgment of a failure !

He recruited and drilled a little force in Kansas where he was so well known, some twenty men ; and when they were ready informed them, for the first time, that the field of action was to be in Virginia, at Harper's Ferry, where was a large and well-stocked armoury, of which as a preliminary he sought to have possession. The attempt, over-daring as it seemed to sound judgment, was for the moment successful. He obtained, by a sudden attack, possession of the armoury, and made a number of prisoners to be held as hostages, or to be freed when by writing to their friends they could give him " a negro man a-piece as ransom." Then the attempt fell through. The negroes, save the heroic five of Brown's band, had none of the qualities necessary for even beginning a war of insurrection, and there was no time to wait for response, though the town of 5000 inhabitants was in a scare only relieved by the arrival of a detachment of militia from the neighbouring town of Charleston, a detachment too numerous for any possibility of resistance. All that remained for the invaders to do was to bravely defend themselves until most of them were slain, Brown's two sons of the number. The few survivors surrendered to meet as sure a fate. The seizure of the armoury was in the night of October 16, 1859 ; on the 19th Brown, desperately wounded, was a prisoner in Charleston jail.

Deeply exercised in mind must Whittier have been. Much as he hated slavery, he was equally opposed to war ; and how could he, as a consistent Friend, ever seem to approve of an armed rebellion ?   In a letter to Mrs. Child, who after much difficulty had obtained leave to visit the hero in his prison, he wrote :—

" *October* 21*st.*

"My dear Friend,—I was glad to get a line from thee, and glad of the opportunity it affords me and my sister to express our admiration of thy generous sympathy with the brave but, methinks, sadly misguided Captain Brown.   We feel deeply (who does not ?) for the noble-hearted, self-sacrificing old man.   But as friends of peace, as well as believers in the Sermon on the Mount, we dare not lend *any* countenance to such attempts as that at Harper's Ferry.

" I hope in our admiration of the noble traits of John Brown's character, we shall be careful how we encourage a repetition of his rash and ill-judged movement.   Thou and I believe in ' a more excellent way.'   I have just been looking at one of the *pikes* sent here by a friend in Baltimore.   It is not a Christian weapon ; it looks too much like murder.

" God is now putting our non-resistance principles to a severe test.   I hope we shall not give the lie to our life-long professions.   I quite agree with thee that we must judge of Brown by *his* standards ; but at the same time we must be true to our settled convictions, and to the duty we owe to humanity.

"Thou wilt see how difficult it is for me to write as thou request. My heart is too heavy and sorrowful. I cannot write now, and can only *wait*, with fervent prayer that the cause we love may receive no detriment."

Still he could not refrain from the expression of his heart-felt sympathy with the "misguided;" could not but have welcomed the opportunity for such expression, as shown in the following :—

> "John Brown of Ossawatomie
>   Spake on his dying day :
> 'I will not have to shrive my soul
>   A priest in slavery's pay ;
> But let some poor slave-mother
>   Whom I have striven to free
> With her children from the gallows-stair
>   Put up a prayer for me !'
>
> John Brown of Ossawatomie,
>   They led him out to die ;
> And lo ! a poor slave-mother
>   With her little child press'd nigh.
> Then the bold blue eye grew tender,
>   And the old harsh face grew mild,
> As he stoop'd between the jeering ranks
>   And kiss'd the negro's child.
>
> The shadows of his stormy life
>   That moment fell apart ;

> And they who blamed the bloody hand
>   Forgave the loving heart ;
> That kiss from all its guilty means
>   Redeem'd the good intent,
> And round the grisly fighter's hair
>   The martyr's aureole bent."

.   .   .   .

And when war followed, " as echo follows song," Whittier would consistently have left the South to secede, nor have approved of armed defence even for the beloved Union. Nay ! had not Massachusetts herself first spoken of secession from the Union that permitted slavery? He would have let the South go, so clearing the North from participation in the curse. But was not this much the same as the conduct for which he had rebuked the Society, the clearing only of their own skirts ? and cannot we, who are not pledged to non-resistance, perceive that, as in old Æsop's fable of the " Trumpeter taken prisoner," the trumpet-call is but a forespoken approval of the battle? As surely as the far-reaching fire of war sprang from the spark thrown into Southern powder by John Brown's "ill-judged " raid, so surely was that desperate action impelled by such words as those of the poet's "Voices of Freedom," however little he intended them to provoke a bloody arbitrement. After all "In war time," despite all Friends' prejudice, he can but write :—

> "If for the age to come this hour
>   Of trial hath vicarious power,

And, bless'd by Thee, our present pain
Be Liberty's eternal gain,
  Thy will be done !

Strike, Thou the Master, we Thy keys,
The anthem of the destinies !
The minor of Thy loftier strain,
Our hearts shall breathe the old refrain,
  Thy will be done ! "

He had praise for Fremont, who first pointed the
fight to its only right end, by proclaiming, so early as
August, 1861, the freedom of all escaped slaves, a
proceeding the necessity for which was not then apparent
to Lincoln, who annulled the proclamation and removed
Fremont from his command.   Whittier wrote :—

" Thy error, Fremont ! simply was to act
 A brave man's part without the statesman's tact."

And on the same occasion we find, in a letter to Mrs.
Child : "If this war is not for emancipation, it is both
wicked and ridiculous. . . . I am afraid the Government
will tie up the hands of Fremont.   I was just thinking of
trying to thank him for his noble word 'free,' when the
papers this morning bring us Lincoln's letter to him,
repudiating the grand utterance.   Well, if the confiscated
slaves are *not* free, then the Government has turned
slaveholder ; that is all.

"I am sick of politicians.   I know and appreciate the
great difficulties in the way of the Administration, but I

see neither honesty nor worldly wisdom in attempting to ignore *the cause of the trouble.*

"They tell us we must trust and have patience ; and I do not like to find fault with the Administration, as in so doing I *seem* to take sides with the secession-sympathisers of the North.

"I thank thee for thy anecdotes of the 'contrabands.' If I can do anything, in prose or verse, to aid the cause, I shall be glad.

"I wish somebody would write a song worthy of the people and the cause ; I am not able to do it."

This letter shows the mental attitude of the man, hampered only by the illogical theory of non-resistance. So he wrote but few war poems, and those with hardly the old fire, rather resigned as regarded the contest, but trusting and hopeful for the result. Beside the lines to Fremont, we have "At Port Royal," in which is the Song of the Negro Boatmen, "Mithridates at Chios," the "Battle Autumn of 1862," an "Anniversary Poem" for the annual Friends' Meeting at Newport in 1863, some few others, and one brave, deservedly popular ballad, "Barbara Frietchie," of an old woman of Frederick Town, Maryland, who is said to have persistently displayed, from an upper window, the Union flag, in the face of Stonewall Jackson and a rebel force passing through the street in which she lived.

Of the departure of regiments, the pomp and circumstance of war, we see nothing in Whittier's poems. His abhorrence of slaughter was innate, and continued by the man's firm convictions ; and the splendour of the movement of vast masses, so purposed, had no charm for the peace-loving Quaker. But when the 54th Massachusetts coloured regiment went forth, headed by its youthful colonel, Robert G. Shaw, he wrote to Mrs. Child: "I shall never forget the scene. As Colonel Shaw rode at the head of his troops, the flower of grace and chivalry, he seemed to me beautiful and awful as an angel of God come down to lead the hosts of freedom to victory." Shaw fell at the assault on Fort Wagner, and was buried there "among his niggers." There is a fine portrait of him by his father's friend, the American painter, William Page. "I have longed," continues Whittier, "to speak the emotions of that hour, but I dared not, lest I should give a new impulse to the war." The Berserker heritage has not been quite effaced, however overlaid by honest Quaker principle.

During this period, in war-time, 1863, there occurred a memorable celebration of the thirtieth anniversary of the founding of the American Anti-Slavery Society at Philadelphia. Garrison, who had presided at the founding, presided here, and in an impressive speech led all to see the signs of approaching triumph. He spoke of Whittier, unable on account of ill-health to attend the meeting; and, before reading a letter sent to account for the poet's non-attendance, spoke of him as one "known and honoured throughout the civilised world." He added: "I have no words to express my sense of the value of his services. There are few living who have done so much to operate upon the public mind and conscience and heart of our country for the abolition of slavery as John Greenleaf Whittier."

Whittier's letter, of course sharing in the congratulations, did not fail to impress the still urgent need of speech. "We must not forget that from this hour new and mighty responsibilities devolve upon us, to aid, direct, and educate these millions, left free indeed, but bewildered, ignorant, naked, and foodless, in the wild chaos of civil war. We have to undo the accumulated wrongs of two centuries; to remake the manhood that slavery has well-nigh unmade; to see to it that the long-oppressed coloured man has a fair field for development and improvement, and to tread under our feet the last vestige of that hateful prejudice which has been the strongest external support of Southern slavery. We must lift ourselves at once to the true Christian attitude where all distinctions of black and white are overlooked in the heartfelt recognition of the brotherhood of man.

"I must not close this letter without confessing that I cannot be sufficiently thankful to the Divine Providence which, in a great measure through thy instrumentality," (the letter is addressed to Garrison) "turned me so early away from what Roger Williams calls 'the world's great trinity, pleasure, profit, and honour,' to take side with the poor and oppressed. I am not insensible to literary reputation; I love, perhaps too well, the praise and good-will of my fellow-men; but I set a higher value on my name as appended to the Anti-Slavery Declaration of 1833 than on the title-page of any book.

"Looking over a life marked by many errors and shortcomings, I rejoice that I have been able to maintain the pledge of that signature, and that in the long intervening years

' My voice, though not the loudest, has been heard
  Wherever Freedom raised her cry of pain.'

Let me, through thee, extend a warm greeting to the
friends, whether of our own or the new generation, who
may assemble on the occasion of commemoration. For
thyself, I need not say that the love and esteem of early
boyhood have lost nothing by the test of time."

On the New Year of 1864 the President's proclamation
declared American slavery to be at an end.

CHAPTER XIII.

POEMS, in no wise war poems, but produced during the war, were "Cobbler Keezar's Vision," "Amy Wentworth," the "Countess," "Andrew Rykman's Prayer," and the "River Path." Now the great strife is at an end the poet may with clear conscience devote himself to art, and, if need be, more fully vindicate his position as a poet, though all of old patriotic utterance be forgotten by peace-loving ears. In 1865 appeared a "Winter Idyll," since better known as "Snowbound," the most perfect, looked at artistically, of the poet's work, from which has already been quoted the description of the poet's family, and from which there is no need to borrow more to show that the poet, released from his self-imposed task of so many years, has at last come to the natural bent of his genius. Now, no need of clangour or the high-voicing of indignant appeal, we have him in the pleasantness of his early home, or among poetic friends, striking the sweet chords of his lyre, well-tuned and free from discord. This "Winter Idyll" fixed his rank beside the best. The "Tent on the Beach" followed in 1867 to enhance his popularity. The pur-pose of this poem is to serve as a sort of frame to poems already written. The occasion is the encampment of Whittier with two friends, the poet Bayard Taylor and the

publisher James T. Fields, on Salisbury Beach; and the
tales of old which they are supposed to hear are the
"Wreck of Rivermouth," the "Grave by the Lake," the
"Brother of Mercy," the "Changeling," the "Maids of
Attetash," "Kallunborg Church," the "Dead Ship of
Harpswell," the "Palatine," and "Abraham Davenport,"
many of which had appeared, at wide intervals, in the
Atlantic Monthly, now grouped together with intervening
descriptions of the grey beach and neighbouring sea-folk,
and many other touches of a true poet's plastic hand. A
few words of himself, as the reader of the tales to his two
companions, are interestingly characteristic.

> "And one there was, a dreamer born,
>   Who, with a mission to fulfil,
>   Had left the Muses' haunts to turn
>   The crank of an opinion mill,
>   Making his rustic reed of song
>   A weapon in the war with Wrong,
> Yoking his fancy to the breaking plough
> That beam-deep turn'd the soil for truth to spring
>   and grow.
>
>   Too quiet seem'd the man to ride
>   The winged Hippogriff, Reform;
>   Was his a voice from side to side
>   To pierce the tumult of the storm?
>   A silent, shy, peace-loving man,
>   He seem'd no fiery partisan
> To hold his way against the public frown,
> The ban of Church and State, the fierce mob's
>   hounding down.

> For while he wrought with strenuous will
>   The work his hands had found to do,
> He heard the fitful music still
>   Of winds that out of dreamland blew;
> The din about him could not drown
> What the strange voices whisper'd down."

Some "National Lyrics" keep up the interest in the issues of the war: the "Mantle of St. John de Matha," "What the Birds said," "Laus Deo," the "Peace Autumn," and lines "to the Thirty-ninth Congress." "Laus Deo" is an exultant song on hearing the bells ring for the passage of the Constitutional Amendment, finally abolishing slavery.

.   .   .   .   .   .

> "Ring, O bells!
> Every stroke exulting tells
> Of the burial hour of Crime.
>   Loud and long that all may hear,
>   Ring for every listening ear
> Of Eternity and Time!

.   .   .   .   .   .

> Loud and long
> Lift the old exulting song!
> Sing with Miriam by the sea:
>   He has cast the mighty down;
>   Horse and rider sink and drown;
> He hath triumph'd gloriously.

.   .   .   .   .   .

> Ring and swing,
>   Bells of joy !   On morning's wing
> Send the song of praise abroad !
>   With a sound of broken chains,
>   Tell the nations that He reigns
> Who alone is Lord and God ! "

The "Peace Autumn" has the same thankful motive. The lines "to the Thirty-ninth Congress" are an earnest appeal for a wise use of victory, for equal laws for black and white, and amnesty for the conquered.

The Occasional Poems that follow are characterised by such intense religious feeling as animated the primitive Christians.   One, "To Bryant on his Birthday," is a generous tribute from poet to poet ; and that "to Thomas Starr King," the Californian preacher, recognises the services of a man to whose influence it was greatly owing that California stayed in the Union.

"Among the Hills" (published in 1868 with other poems) is a love-story, of a city-bred lady and a farmer lover,—simple, yet rich in pictorial touches. In the series with it may be noticed a ballad, the "Dole of Jarl Thorkell," the "Clear Vision," the "Two Rabbis," the "Meeting" (a Quaker Meeting), and "Freedom in Brazil."

"Miriam," containing the story of "the good Shah Akbar," appeared in 1870, with "Norembega," "Nauhaught (the Indian Deacon), "Garibaldi," and the lovely idyll, "In School Days," too perfect for even a part of it to be omitted.

"Still sits the schoolhouse by the road,
　　A ragged beggar sunning;
Around it still the sumachs grow,
　　And blackberry vines are running.

Within, the master's desk is seen,
　　Deep-scarr'd by raps official;
The warping floor, the batter'd seats,
　　The jack-knife's carved initial;

The charcoal frescoes on the wall;
　　The door's worn sill, betraying
The feet that, creeping slow to school,
　　Went storming out to playing.

Long years ago a winter sun
　　Shone over it at setting;
Lit up its western window-panes,
　　And low eaves' icy fretting.

It touch'd the tangled golden curls,
　　And brown eyes full of grieving,
Of one who still her steps delay'd
　　When all the school were leaving.

For near her stood the little boy
　　Her childish favour singled,
His cap pull'd low upon a face
　　Where pride and shame were mingled.

Pushing with restless feet the snow
  To right and left, he linger'd,—
As restlessly her tiny hands
  The blue-check'd apron finger'd.

He saw her lift her eyes, he felt
  The soft hand's light caressing,
And heard the tremble of her voice,
  As if a fault confessing.

' I'm sorry that I spelt the word ;
  I hate to go above you :
Because,'—the brown eyes lower fell,—
  ' Because, you see, I love you.'

Still memory to a grey-hair'd man
  That sweet child-face is showing.
Dear girl ! the grasses on her grave
  Have forty years been growing.

He lives to learn, in life's hard school,
  How few who pass above him
Lament their triumph and his loss,
  Like her, because they love him."

The "Pennsylvania Pilgrim" (1872) is a quiet sketch
of the German jurist and scholar, Francis Daniel
Pastorius, who at the invitation of Penn led a colony of
German Pietists to settle near Philadelphia, there founding Germantown. A long prose preface by Whittier gives
account of the proceeding, noting especially his memorial
against slavery in 1688, adopted by the Germantown

Friends, and sent up to the monthly meeting; remarkable as the first protest made by a religious body against Negro Slavery. "The Pilgrims of Plymouth," writes Whittier in this preface, "have not lacked historian or poet. Justice has been done to their faith, courage, and self-sacrifice, and to the mighty influence of their endeavours to establish righteousness on the earth. The Quaker Pilgrims of Pennsylvania, seeking the same object by different means, have not been equally fortunate. The power of their testimony for truth and holiness, peace and freedom, enforced only by what Milton calls 'the unresistible might of meekness,' has been felt through two centuries in the amelioration of penal severities, the abolition of slavery, the reform of the erring, the relief of the poor and suffering,—felt, in brief, in every step of human progress. But of the men themselves, with the single exception of William Penn, scarcely anything is known. Contrasted, from the outset, with the stern, aggressive Puritans of New England, they have come to be regarded as 'a feeble folk,' with a personality as doubtful as their unregarded graves. They were not soldiers, like Miles Standish; they had no figure so picturesque as Vane; no leader so rashly brave and haughty as Endicott. No Cotton Mather wrote their *Magnalia;* they had no awful drama of supernaturalism in which Satan and his angels were actors ; and the only witch mentioned in their simple annals was a poor old Swedish woman who, on complaint of her countrywomen, was tried and acquitted of everything but imbecility and folly. Nothing but common-place offices of civility came to pass between them and the Indians ; indeed their enemies taunted them with the fact that the savages did not regard them as Christians, but just such men as themselves. Yet it must be apparent to every careful observer of the progress of American civilisation that its two principal currents had their sources in the entirely opposite directions of the Puritan and Quaker colonies. . . .

"In the poem I have attempted nothing beyond a study of the life and times of the Pennsylvania colonist, a simple picture of a noteworthy man and his locality."

The "Singer," in the same volume, refers to the sisters Alice and Phœbe Cary, of Cincinnati, Ohio, both writers in the *National Era* while Whittier was connected with it, both known as pleasant versifiers since,—Alice, the elder, the more popular, though, as it seems to the present writer, Phœbe's fewer verses showed a glint of a higher faculty. Among other poems here are "King Volmer and Elsie" (a ballad from the Danish), "Marguerite" (also a ballad), and "The Sisters," of a difference from Whittier's subjects, to be noticed. It reads as if it might be from the old French, a ballad which Dante Rossetti might have written.

"Annie and Rhoda, sisters twain,
  Woke in the night to the sound of rain,

The rush of wind, the ramp and roar,
  Of great waves climbing a rocky shore.

Annie rose up in her bedgown white,
  And look'd out into the storm and night.

'Hush, and hearken!' she cried in fear,
  'Hearest thou nothing? sister dear!'"

' I hear the sea and the plash of rain,
And roar of the north-east hurricane.

'Get thee back to the bed so warm !
No good comes of watching a storm.

'What is it to thee, I fain would know,
That waves are roaring and wild winds blow?'

'No lover of thine is afloat to miss
The harbour lights on a night like this.'

' But I heard a voice cry out my name :
Up from the sea on the wind it came.

'Twice and thrice have I heard it call ;
And the voice is the voice of Estwick Hall.'

On the pillow the sister toss'd her head :
'Hall of the Heron is safe,' she said.

' In the tautest schooner that ever swam
He rides at anchor in Anisquam.

'And, if in peril from swamping sea
Or lee shore rocks, would he call on thee?'

But the girl heard only the wind and tide,
And wringing her small white hands she cried—

'O sister Rhoda ! there's something wrong :
I hear it again, so loud and long.

'Annie! Annie! I hear it call,
And the voice is the voice of Estwick Hall.'

Up sprang the elder with eyes aflame;
'Thou liest! he never would call thy name.

'If he did, I would pray the wind and sea
To keep him for ever from thee and me.'

Then out of the sea blew a dreadful blast:
Like the cry of a dying man it pass'd.

The young girl hush'd on her lips a groan,
But through her tears a strange light shone:

The solemn joy of her heart's release
To own and cherish its love in peace.

'Dearest!' she whisper'd under breath,
'Life was a lie, but true is death.

'The love I hid from myself away
Shall crown me now in the light of day.

'My ears shall never to wooer list,
Never by lover my lips be kiss'd.

'Sacred to thee am I henceforth,
Thou in heaven and I on earth.'

She came and stood by her sister's bed;
'Hall of the Heron is dead!' she said.

'The wind and the waves their work have done,
We shall see him no more beneath the sun.

'Little will reck that heart of thine,
It loved him not with a love like mine.

'I for his sake, were he but here,
Could hem and broider thy bridal gear ;

'Though hands should tremble and eyes be wet,
And stitch for stitch in my heart be set.

'But now my soul with his soul I wed :
Thine the living, and mine the dead.'"

In 1875, the poet in his sixty-eighth year, Whittier published a collection of sixteen poems under the title of "Hazel Blossoms": not the blossoms of the nut tree, but of the witch (properly wych) hazel found in damp forests throughout the United States, and renowned for its reputed power, in efficient hands, of indicating subterranean water-springs. The principal poem is a stately eulogy, in fifty four-line stanzas, on "Charles Sumner," who died in 1874. In a "Sea-Dream" is the revelation of a long-hidden sorrow, scarcely hinted at through all his songs. But what else can mean such words as these ?

"But turn to me thy dear girl-face
        Without the angel's crown,
    The wedded roses of thy lips,
        Thy loose hair rippling down
        In waves of golden brown !

Look forth once more through space and time,
　　And let thy sweet shade fall
In tenderest grace of soul and form
　　On memory's frescoed wall,
　　A shadow and yet all !

　　.　　　　.　　　　.　　　　.　　　　.

At breakfast hour the singer read
　　The city news, with comment wise.

　　.　　　　.　　　　.　　　　.　　　　.

No word betray'd the mystery fine
　　That trembled on the singer's tongue ;
He came and went, and left no sign
　　Behind him, save the song he sung."

To the "Hazel Blossoms" Whittier appended " Poems
by Elizabeth H. Whittier," nine poems, of similar bearing
and with an excellence not unworthy to be echoes of her
brother's muse.

"Mabel Martin," an amplification of the "Witch's
Daughter," was published with illustrations in 1874.

May a man of seventy ("threescore years and ten")
write a love-song ?　We shall see in the "Henchman":

" My lady walks her morning round,
　　My lady's page her fleet greyhound ;
　　My lady's hair the fond winds stir,
　　And all the birds make songs for her.

　　Her thrushes sing in Rathburn bowers,
　　And Rathburn side is gay with flowers ;

But ne'er like hers, in flower or bird,
Was beauty seen or music heard.

The distance of the stars is hers ;
The least of all her worshippers,
The dust beneath her dainty heel,
She knows not that I see or feel.

O proud and calm ! she cannot know
Where'er she goes with her I go ;
O cold and fair ! she cannot guess
I kneel to share her hound's caress.

Gay knights beside her hunt and hawk,
I rob their ears of her sweet talk ;
Her suitors come from east and west,
I steal her smiles from every guest.

Unheard of her, in loving words
I greet her with the song of birds ;
I reach her with her green-arm'd bowers,
I kiss her with the lips of flowers.

The hound and I are on her trail,
The wind and I uplift her veil ;
As if the calm, cold moon she were,
And I the tide, I follow her.

As unrebuked as they, I share
The license of the sun and air,
And in a common homage hide
My worship from her scorn and pride.

World-wide apart, and yet so near,
I breathe her charmed atmosphere,
Wherein to her my service brings
The reverence due to holy things.

Her maiden pride, her haughty name,
My dumb devotion shall not shame;
The love that no return doth crave
To knightly levels lifts the slave.

No lance have I, in joust or fight
To splinter in my lady's sight;
But at her feet how blest were I
For any need of hers to die."

It has all the grace and genuineness of Sidney. What might he not have written in the eager passionate days of his young manhood! Yet even for such pure love-lyrics as this we would not part with his "Voices of Freedom," lower as they may rank as only poetry, and wanting often the perfectness of poetic art. The "Henchman" appears in the volume of 1878, preceded by the "Vision of Echard," the vision of a Benedictine monk of Marsburg, who heard the voice of God with respect to the traditional forms of worship and the real service of the heart. It is an excellent homily upon spiritual things, conceived in an exalted mood and expressed with vigour. Every stanza, and almost every line, is worth quoting for power of speech or nobility of sentiment. Age had not weakened the poet's power. Here are a few stanzas out of forty-nine.

.   .   .   .   .   .

" I loathe your wrangling councils,
　　I tread upon your creeds :
Who made ye mine avengers,
　　Or told you of my needs ?

　　　.　　　.　　　.　　　.

No more from rocky Horeb
　　The smitten waters gush ;
Fallen is Bethel's ladder,
　　Quench'd is the burning bush.

　　　.　　　.　　　.　　　.

No more in ark or hill-grove
　　The Holiest abides ;
Not in the scroll's dead letter
　　The eternal secret hides.

　　　.　　　.　　　.　　　.

What if the earth is hiding
　　Her old faiths, long outworn,
What is it to the Changeless Truth
　　That yours shall fail in turn ?

　　　.　　　.　　　.　　　.

Still in perpetual judgment
　　I hold assize within,
With sure reward of holiness
　　And dread rebuke of sin.

　　　.　　　.　　　.　　　.

The stern behest of duty,
　　The doom-book open thrown,
The heaven ye seek, the hell ye fear,
　　Are with yourselves alone."

　　.　　　.　　　.　　　.　　　.　　　.

The "Witch of Wenham," in sixty stanzas, is a ballad, as of old ballad days; based on a colonial tradition, the scene laid by the Lake of Naumkeag, now known as Wenham, famed both in America and in England for the purity of its ice.

"Sunset on the Bearcamp" is a magnificent verse-landscape, one of the finest of Whittier's descriptive poems. The "Seeking of the Waterfall" is of the same character: a series of beautiful scenes of rocks and brooks, wild woods, and granite ledges, leading to the sublime and inaccessible. The "Sunset" may be quoted from as example of this special phase of the poet's genius.

> "A gold fringe on the purpling hem
>   Of hills the river runs
> As down its long green valley falls
>   The last of summer's suns.
> Along its tawny gravel bed,
>   Broad-flowing, swift, and still,
> As if its meadow levels felt
>   The hurry of the hill,
> Noiseless between its banks of green
>   From curve to curve it slips;
> The drowsy maple-shadows rest
>   Like fingers on its lips.
>
> A waif from Carroll's wildest hills,
>   Unstoried and unknown,
> The ursine legend of its name
>   Prowls on its banks alone.

Yet flowers as fair its slopes adorn
　　As ever Yarrow knew,
Or, under rainy Irish skies,
　　By Spenser's Mulla grew ;
And through the gaps of leaning trees
　　Its mountain cradle shows,
The gold against the amethyst,
　　The green against the rose.

Touch'd by a light that hath no name,
　　A glory never sung,
Aloft on sky and mountain wall
　　Are God's great pictures hung.
How changed the summits vast and old !
　　No longer granite-brow'd,
They melt in rosy mist ; the rock
　　Is softer than the cloud.
The valley holds its breath ; no leaf
　　Of all its elms is twirl'd :
The silence of eternity
　　Seems falling on the world.

The pause before the breaking seals
　　Of mystery is this ;
Yon miracle play of night and day
　　Makes dumb its witnesses.
What unseen altar crowns the hills
　　That reach up stair on stair ?
What eyes look through, what white wings fan
　　These purple veils of air ?

What Presence from the heavenly heights
  To those of earth stoops down ?
Not vainly Hellas dream'd of Gods
  On Ida's snowy crown.

Slow fades the vision of the sky,
  The golden water pales,
And over all the valley land
  A grey-wing'd vapour sails.
I go the common way of all ;
  The sunset fires will burn,
The flowers will blow, the rivers flow,
  When I no more return.
No whisper from the mountain pine,
  No lapsing stream shall tell
The stranger, treading where I tread,
  Of him who loved them well.

Past beauty seen is never lost,
  God's colours all are fast ;
The glory of this sunset heaven
  Into my soul has pass'd."

.   .   .   .   .

Harking back to earlier days, "In the Old South"
he tells of the poor crazed enthusiast, called upon, as she
believed, to bear testimony against the unchristian conduct of the Puritan oppressors of the Friends.

" She came and stood in the Old South Church,
  A wonder and a sign,
With a look the old-time Sybils wore,
  Half crazed and half divine.

Save the mournful sackcloth about her wound,
　　Unclothed as the primal mother,
With limbs that trembled and eyes that blazed
　　With a fire she dare not smother.

Loose on her shoulders fell her hair
　　With sprinkled ashes grey;
She stood in the broad aisle strange and weird
　　As a soul at the judgment day."

Contrast this, as showing the various power and multiform production of a great poet, with the "Henchman," and with the charming idyll "In School Days," or with that most perfect perhaps of all idylls, "Telling the Bees," an earlier poem, reserved for later comment.

In this same volume we have the "Centennial Hymn;" the "Library" (written for the opening of a free public library at Haverhill); the "Two Angels,"— "The loveliest one was Pity, the dearest one was Love;" —"King Solomon and the Ants" (telling how the great king turned his cavalcade aside so as not to crush an ant-hill in his way, one of several poems for children), with the wise moral still somewhere needed, the remark of the Queen of Sheba :—

　　　　"Happy must be the State
　　　　　　Whose ruler heedeth more
　　　　　　The murmurs of the poor
　　　　　Than flatteries of the great."

"At Eventide" (a retrospect), the "King's Missive" (for the release of the imprisoned Quakers, a poem which led to a renewal of discussion between the friends of the Puritan and those of the Quakers, as to its historical value), the "Lost Occasion" (a generous tribute to Daniel Webster), "Abram Morrison," the "Minister's Daughter," and other poems not unworthy of the old poet, complete this volume of 1878.

Allusion has already been made to his hymns. Hymn-book makers have had in his religious poems a very quarry for their exploiting. Hymn-tinkers, too, have not failed, after their manner, to adapt them when in their view not quite suitable. The "Plymouth Collection," so early as 1865, printed eleven; Longfellow and Johnson's "Hymns of the Spirit," 1864, has as many as twenty-two; the "Unitarian Hymn and Tune Book," 1868, has seven; and Dr. Martineau's "Hymns of Praise," 1874, has seven also.

Beside his own poems for children, such as "King Solomon and the Ants," "Red Riding Hood," and the "Robin," Whittier compiled two books of selections for children. Another compilation, "Songs of Three Centuries," 1876, shows his predilections with regard to his fellow-poets. Among them we note Wordsworth's "Intimations of Immortality," and "Ode to Duty," Coleridge's "Christabel," Shelley's "To a Skylark," Keats' "Eve of St. Agnes," Elliott's "Forest Worship," Hood's "Song of the Shirt" and "Ruth," Mrs. Browning's "A Musical Instrument," Browning's "Lost Leader," Tennyson's "Mariana," Thackeray's "At the Church-Gate," Emerson's "Apology," Longfellow's "Psalm of Life" and "Paul Revere's Ride," Lowell's "Commemoration Ode" and the "Courtin'." Of his own verse he has preferred the " Grave by the Lake " (from the " Tent on the Beach "), "My Birthday," "The Vanishers," " In School Days," " Laus Deo," and " The Eve of Election," the most with still the preacher-purpose.

His last words in the "complete edition " of 1882, Houghton, Miffin, & Co., are a characteristically modest acknowledgment of the popularity of his works.

" Beside that milestone where the level sun,
   Nigh unto setting, sheds his last, low rays
On word and work irrevocably done,
   Life's blending threads of good and ill outspun,
I hear, O friends ! your words of cheer and praise,
Half-doubtful if myself or otherwise ;
Like him who in the old Arabian joke
A beggar slept, and crowned Caliph woke.

Thanks not the less !   With not unglad surprise
I see my life-work through your partial eyes ;
Assured in giving to my home-taught songs
A higher value than of right belongs,
You do but read within the written lines
The finer grace of unfulfill'd designs."

"At Sundown "—printed only for friends and sent to them on his eightieth birthday, in 1890, and published since his death with some additions, making a collection of eighteen poems—completes our record of a life's work. The dainty and affectionate dedication in this is to the poet Stedman.   The eighteen poems are :—

The " Christmas of 1888 ; " the " Vow of Washington " (1889, read at the Contennial Celebration of the

Inauguration of the First President); the "Captain's Well" (a ballad); "An Outdoor Reception," "R.S.S. at Deer Island on the Merrimac," "Burning Drift-wood," "James Russell Lowell," "Haverhill" (read out at the celebration of the 250th anniversary of the city, July 2, 1890)—

> " The singer of a farewell rhyme
> Upon whose utmost verge of time
> The shades of night are falling down,
> I pray God bless the good old town."

"To G. G." (a daughter of Daniel Gurton, delegate from Haverhill, England, to the celebration at Haverhill, Massachusetts), he writes—

> " Say that our love survives the severing strain ;
> That the New England, with the Old, holds fast
> The proud, fond memories of a common past ;
> Unbroken still the ties of blood remain."

The remaining contents are, "Inscription" for a bas-relief representing the last Indian and the last bison, carved on a boulder in Denver Park, Colorado ; "To Lydia H. Sigourney ;" "On a Memorial Tablet ;" "Milton" (on the memorial window in St. Margaret's Church, Westminster); the "Birthday Wreath," Dec. 17, 1891 ; the "Wind of March," "To Oliver Wendell Holmes," "Between the Gates," and the "Last Eve of Summer." In the reprint, the latest writing "To Oliver Wendell Holmes," on that old friend's eighty-third birth-day, bears date of "8th mo. 29th" (August 29, 1892), but nine days before the writer passed away. His last words were wise and helpful :—

.　　.　　.　　.

" The gift is thine the weary world to make
　　More cheerful for thy sake,
Soothing the ears its Miserere pains
　　With the old Hellenic strains,

Lighting the sullen face of discontent
　　With smiles for blessings sent.
Enough of selfish wailing has been had ;
　　Thank God for notes more glad !

Life is indeed no holiday ; therein
　　Are want and woe and sin,
Death and its nameless fears, and over all
　　Our pitying tears must fall.

Sorrow is real ; but the counterfeit,
　　Which folly brings to it,
We need thy wit and wisdom to resist,
　　O rarest Optimist !

Thy hand, old Friend ! the service of our days
　　In differing moods and ways,
May prove to those who follow in our train
　　Not valueless nor vain."

.　　.　　.　　.

A fair rebuke to the crowds of minor verse-makers
and to the fashion of personal poetic moaning to which
his own brave and cheerful spirit had never conde-
scended ; a fine appreciation also of the friend whose
manner of work has been so different from his own.

For nearly all his life Whittier had been in poor health, the overwork of his early journalistic days having brought on neuralgia and headache, so that through many years he could not write for fifteen minutes at a time without headache. Indeed, he was in but delicate health for almost all his life—a serious hindrance to continuous mental exertion. Watchfulness and care, however, greatly benefited his condition during his later years.

For a few days before his death our poet had begun to fail. Still it was thought that the quiet of a restful visit to Elmwood, the house of his friend, Miss Sarah A. Gove, at Hampton Falls, almost within sight of Rivermouth, might give him some reprieve. But a stroke of paralysis on the 3rd of September deprived him of the use of one arm and affected the muscles of the throat, so that, unable to swallow, he was prevented from taking nourishment. He passed peacefully away on Wednesday, the 7th of December, 1892, able, even to the last, to recognise the friends around him.

In the early afternoon of Saturday, December 10, the funeral services were held at Amesbury, in the old-fashioned homestead where he so long resided, now the residence of Judge Cote. Its doors were opened to hundreds. The members of the City Government of Haverhill attended in a body. Both in Amesbury and Haverhill shops were closed, and business was generally suspended during the services; at the same time also in Danvers, where much of his later years had been spent. Flags were lowered to half-staff. The burial words were spoken by friends in the garden of what had been his own Amesbury house ; Edmund Clarence Stedman, the younger poet and reverential and esteemed friend of Whittier, was the last speaker. The surviving members of the Hutchinson family (not forgotten as singers in England) closed the services with a hymn. Among the pall-bearers were the Rev. Samuel J. May (the old abolitionist comrade), Stedman, and the poetess Lucy Larcom. Fresh roses were laid upon the coffin; and the grave, in the meeting-house yard, was lined with ferns and golden rod. It was a fit burial for one not only admired and reverenced, but deeply loved. And it was according to his own desire, expressed in his will, dated February 11, 1890 :—

"It is my wish that my funeral may be conducted in the plain and quiet way of the Society of Friends, with which I was connected, not only by birthright but also by a settled conviction of the truth of its principles and the importance of its testimonies."

Of the Society of Friends he was always a faithful member, though never narrow or technical in his spirit. In his younger time his anti-slavery associations sometimes brought him into danger of discipline, and he used to say, jokingly, in his later years, that the Society would gladly have then put upon him, would he have consented, all the committee work and the little dignities from which his position as a reformer had excluded him. He always held to the prescribed garb, so far as the cut of his coat was concerned, but conformed to the ways of the world in his other attire.

The poet died not poor. Hard struggles and scarcity marked his early years ; but when, after 1857, his poetic genius could be appreciated, despite the first offensiveness of the earnest Abolitionist, he rose quickly in public favour. In and from 1883 his publishers bought his copyrights, then existing and for the future, at the same rate as they paid to Longfellow and Lowell—$5,000 (£1,000) a year. Probably, with his simple habits, and having some other means, he spent little or nothing of this. So he was able to leave bequests—to a niece who had lived with him at Amesbury after his sister's death, now Mrs. J. Packard, to her and her husband (the editor of the *Portland Argus*, by whom his biography is to be written) the sum of $20,000 (or £4,000), and about twice that sum among other relatives, nephews and nieces, besides considerable, but smaller, charitable bequests.

For his epitaph can better or more characteristic words be written than those of his fellow poet, Lowell, sent from England in 1884 ?

" Peaceful by birthright as a virgin lake,
    The lily's anchorage, which no eyes behold
 Save those of stars, yet for thy brothers' sake,
    That lay in bonds, thou blew'st a blast as bold
 As that wherewith the heart of Roland brake,
    Far heard through Pyrenean valleys old."

CHAPTER XIV.

A ND now, what place among poets, judged solely
and strictly as a poet, must we allot to this writer
of nearly four hundred poems—not counting the lost,
nor such as he himself struck from his list as unworthy
of preservation ? In so great a number we, of course,
can but note great difference of quality. A large proportion of the "Voices of Freedom" may be mere
improvisation, uttered, hardly to be said composed,
on the spur of the occasion, with the passionate purpose
of immediately reaching the hearts of his readers, with
neither time nor care for consideration of artistic perfectness. The impulse which gave birth to them was,
indeed, patriotic rather than poetic : so, however good
the declamatory verse, it was often to be classed as
rhetoric rather than poetry. But after any deduction on
such ground there is enough, even in these first outbursts,
and leaving aside what he did when he reached his full
stature, to show the true and gifted poet, sure to find at
last, in his own country, but compeers and no superiors.
If in days when he took up his lyre in the haste of
apostolic fervour he sometimes did not wait to tune it,
it was not that he could not have done so, but the notes

had to be promptly struck, even though the music were dissonant. He was a poet still, for all shortcomings, for all faults of expression, though in those days of warfare the preacher hid the artist.

And, in truth, his verse has somewhat suffered from this haste, sometimes, but not frequently. We find one most ungrammatical line in the "Knight of St. John ":—

"Closed o'er my steed and I ;"

we get *Romance* and *allies* accented on the first syllable ; such misrhymes as *Parle* and *Basle*, *worn* and *turn*, *court* and *dirt*, *joins* and *pines*, *faults* and *revolts*, *flood* and *Hood*, *even* and *Devon*, *heaven* and *forgiven*, and such like, not only in the hastiest work. Slight ear or eye sores these, when we are thinking of wide well-earned fame, and perhaps to be accounted for also by the lack of early musical training, the poet having been brought up at a period when Friends disapproved of music ; or by some want of natural endowment which limited the range of his verse, and made him prefer, even in later days, the simple strains of the four-line ballad. This he could make not only effective, but melodious. How much of any want of melody anywhere may be accounted for by his own statement in 1882—"I don't know one tune from another " ! Conscious of lacking a certain faculty when using an unusual licence in "Pulse o' the Midnight Beating," he falls back, under editorial snub-bing, into the old foot-rule measure. Something, too, may have arisen from want of health, and composition under sorrowful or painful circumstances. Even "Snowbound " was written " to beguile the weariness of a sick chamber." Make any allowance for the consequences of such hinderings, and for time taken from the quiet study of his art to be devoted to the manful service of Humanity, there is but little, while we the more love and reverence the man, to lessen the admiration due to him as one of the greater lords of song.

It is indeed a fair question whether the poet lost or gained by his early abnegation. That he himself felt he had given up something appears in the apologetic Proem, written in 1847, prefixed to the edition of 1876, the expression of a thought of dissatisfaction (the dissatisfaction of every true artist) with what he had accomplished on strictly poetic ground. He owns :—

" I love the old melodious lays
Which softly melt the ages through,
　The songs of Spenser's golden days,
　Arcadian Sidney's silvery phrase,
Sprinkling our noon of time with freshest morning dew.

　Yet vainly in my quiet hours
To breathe their marvellous notes I try ;
　I feel them, as the leaves and flowers
　In silence feel the dewy showers,
And drink with glad still lips the blessing of the sky

　The rigour of a frozen clime,
The harshness of an untaught ear,
　The jarring words of one whose rhyme
　Beat often Labour's hurried time
On Duty's rugged march through storm and strife, are
　　here.

Of mystic beauty, dreamy grace,
No rounded art the lack supplies ;
　　Unskill'd the subtler lines to trace
　　Or softer shades of Nature's face,
I view her common forms with unanointed eyes.

Nor mine the seer-like power to show
The secrets of the heart and mind,
　　To drop the plummet-line below
　　Our common world of joy and woe,
A more intense despair or brighter hope to find.

Yet here at least an earnest sense
Of human right and weal is shown,
　　A hate of tyranny intense
　　And hearty in its vehemence
As if my brother's pain and sorrow were my own.

O Freedom ! if to me belong
Nor mighty Milton's gift divine,
　　Nor Marvell's wit and graceful song,
　　Still, with a love as deep and strong
As theirs, I lay like them my best gifts on thy shrine."

Yet it seems well said by the writer of the obituary
notice of Whittier in the New York *Nation* that his muse
" most probably gained in all ways from the strong
tonic of the anti-slavery agitation.　That gave a training
in directness, simplicity, genuineness ; it taught him to
shorten his sword, and to produce strong effects by
common means.　It made him permanently high-minded
also, and placed him, as he himself always said, above
the perils and temptations of a merely literary career."

The perils and temptations of a merely literary career : that especially of settling into a low sybaritism, in which all that is cared for or believed in is the artist's (poet's or painter's) own exceeding great pleasure in his work, the self-satisfying acceptance of the mischievous half-truth of " Art for Art's sake," by which so many are bewildered, in which so many are lost ! If it be true that, as the eye sees only what it brings the means of seeing, so nothing can come of nothingness, the culture and growth of the man can but add to the growth and aid the development of the poet. Can we not perceive this, if we may be allowed for a moment to compare our Quaker poet with one, hardly of less natural genius, to whom the name of poet is loudly given, Edgar Allan Poe? In Poe, helped it may be by his native gift, we see the admirable result of much study of words, rhythms, and assonances, mellifluous, meaningless jingles, pleasant to musical ears, this and but little else ; in the other we find high thoughts, noble lessons (of which true poetry—not therefore didactic—is never void), and everywhere the outcome of gentle and heroic thought, preaching to us not as the preacher, but as storm and sunshine, sky and flowers, and the various aspects of grand woods, and the line of mountain beauty preach to us, speaking in masculine music to our souls. The difference between the two poets (the name given to both) is the wide difference between the sound that tickles the ears and the divine word that touches the heart. The fame of Poe as a poet, for all his most bewitching sensuousness, must sink into insignificance beside that of Whittier. Poe's finest and most polished verse is as much inferior to the best of Whittier's as the character of the one man is below that of the other. Of the verse this may indeed be said without any question of moral worth, a question which does not penetrate the fog-region of the critical approver of Art for only Art's sake.

I would say that Whittier lost nothing of the magical power of poetry by his first service in the ranks of patriotism, though that service had been even more of the grudged years of Leah before the heart-gift for Rachel. His love was for the delight of poetry, but the voice of Duty was the stronger, and there was no grudging in his devotion.

May we risk another comparison, even with Wordsworth? He did not attain the heights of Wordsworth's sublimest work ; but on the lower ground, true domain of poetry still, the ground of simplicity, he stands as more than equal.

" We are Seven," the " Pet Lamb," the " Last of the Flock," " Ruth," and some others of their like, of the great poet's work, betray a certain affectation of simplicity not altogether undeserving of the derision which first greeted the " Lake School." They have not the genuine simplicity of Blake, or Burns, which like that of Whittier, is natural, " born not made." " Telling the Bees " may enforce the argument.

> " Here is the place : right over the hill
>   Runs the path I took ;
>   You can see the gap in the old wall still,
>   And the stepping-stones in the shallow brook.

There is the house, with the gate red-barr'd,
    And the poplars tall;
And the barn's brown length, and the cattle-yard,
    And the white horns tossing above the wall.

There are the beehives ranged in the sun;
    And down by the brink
Of the brook are her poor flowers, weed o'errun,
    Pansy and daffodil, rose and pink.

A year has gone, as the tortoise goes,
    Heavy and slow;
And the same rose blows, and the same sun glows,
    And the same brook sings of a year ago.

There's the same sweet clover smell in the breeze;
    And the June sun warm
Tangles his wings of fire in the trees,
    Setting as then over Fernside Farm.

I mind me how, with a lover's care,
    From my Sunday coat
I brush'd off the burrs, and smooth'd my hair,
    And cool'd at the brookside my brow and throat.

Since we parted, a month had pass'd,
    To love a year;
Down through the beeches I look'd at last
    On the little red gate and the well-sweep near.

I can see it all now : the slantwise rain
    Of light through the leaves,
The sun-down's blaze on her window-pane,
    The bloom of her roses under the eaves.

Just the same as a month before,
   The house and the trees,
The barn's brown gable, the vine by the door,—
   Nothing changed but the hives of the bees.

Before them, under the garden wall,
   .Forward and back,
Went, drearily singing, the chore-girl [1] small,
   Draping each hive with a shred of black.

Trembling I listen'd; the summer sun
   Had the chill of snow,—
For I knew she was telling the bees of one
   Gone on the journey we all must go.

Then I said to myself—My Mary weeps
   For the dead to-day;
Haply her blind old grandsire sleeps
   The fret and pain of his age away.

But her dog whined low: on the doorway-sill,
   With his cane to his chin,
The old man sat; and the chore-girl still
   Sang to the bees stealing out and in.

And the song she was singing ever since
   In my ear sounds on:
'Stay at home, pretty bees! fly not hence!
   Mistress Mary is dead and gone.'"

[1] The chores are what in England would be called the work of the charwoman, in New England the chorewoman, or choregirl. The word may have been of Old English use.

" My Playmate," of about the same date as this, and the later " In School Days," already quoted—nor only these—are of the same exquisite texture, songs from the heart, homely and as genuinely natural. Nor, still venturing on a comparison, neither irreverent nor irrelevant, is there anything of the descriptive poetry of Wordsworth more excellent than Whittier's poetry of the Merrimac.

Richard Henry Stoddard (to distinguish him from other literary Stoddards), who now stands highest among American poets, writing of this descriptive verse, and of Whittier's poems of Nature in general, marks them as " characterised by poetic elements which are not common among descriptive poets. They are not enumerative like the landscapes that form the backgrounds of Scott's metrical romances, but suggestive; for though there is an abundance of form and colour in them, their value does not depend upon these qualities so much as upon the luminous atmosphere in which they are steeped. They are more than picturesque in that they reveal the personality of the poet, a personality that, changing with the moods they awaken is always tender and thoughtful, grateful for the glimpses of loveliness they disclose, and consoled by the spiritual truth they teach. What this truth is the readers of Whittier know after reading ' Hampton Beach,' ' A Dream of Summer,' ' On receiving an Eagle's Quill from Lake Superior,' ' The Last Walk in Summer,' or indeed almost any of Whittier's poems of Nature." " A Dream of Summer, 4th of 1st month, 1847," may here instance this.

" Bland as the morning breath of June
  The south-west breezes play ;
And through its haze the winter noon
  Seems warm as summer's day,
The snow-plumed Angel of the North
  Has dropp'd his icy spear ;
Again the mossy earth looks forth,
  Again the streams gush clear.

The fox his hillside cell forsakes,
  The musk-rat leaves his nook,
The bluebird in the meadow brakes
  Is singing with the brook.
Bear up, O Mother Nature ! cry
  Bird, breeze, and streamlet free ;
Our winter voices prophesy
  Of summer days to thee.

Lo, in those winters of the soul,
  By bitter blasts and drear,
O'erswept from Memory's frozen pole,
  Will sunny days appear.
Reviving hope and faith, they show
  The soul its living powers,
And how beneath the winter's snow
  Lie germs of summer flowers.

The Night is mother of the Day,
  The Winter of the Spring ;
And ever upon old Decay
  The greenest mosses cling

Behind the cloud the star-light lurks,
　　Through showers the sunbeams fall ;
For God, who loveth all His works,
　　Has left His Hope with all."

" The personality of Whittier," again borrowing good
words from Stoddard, " which was so pervasive poetically
in his communings with Nature, was touched to deeper
issues when he permitted it to brood upon itself in its
purely human relationships, as he did in poems like
'Memories,' 'My Namesake,' 'The Barefoot Boy,'
'In School Days,' and 'My Birthday.' He was at
his best in 'Snowbound,' which is not only a personal
poem in the sweetest, tenderest, truest sense, but a
national poem in the largest sense, the poem of
the American people " [say certainly of New England]
" in the distinctive sense that 'The Cotter's Saturday
Night' of Burns is the poem of the Scottish people."

Still quoting Mr. Stoddard : " The poetry of Whittier
differs from that of other American poets in several
particulars which will probably be better understood by
those who are to come after us than they have yet been
by ourselves, and which will determine his ultimate
place among nineteenth-century poets who have expressed themselves in the English tongue. It differs
from that of his contemporaries who alone are worthy of
consideration in a serious estimate of our verse in that
it is the natural expression of his individual genius, his
simple, native speech, not a studied literary exercise ;
and that from first to last it has concerned itself with the
life of his countrymen. Why he was born a poet we

can no more tell from what we know of his parentage
and environments than why Burns was ; but he was so
born, as surely as Burns, and it was his only heritage.
His parents were plain people who lived by farming,
which was not a lucrative calling in a small country
town in New England, in the first decade of the century.
They were poor, hard-working, simple-minded folk, of a
more serious turn of mind than most of those about
them, for they were Quakers, but not, it would seem,
the kind of folk to divine the genius of their son, much
less to educate him, for it was necessary that he should
work on the farm, as they did.   They were unlettered,
for, outside of the Bible and the few denominational
writings on their shelves, they were not readers; these,
the county newspaper and the 'Farmers' Almanac'
were Whittier's library, the common school in winter
being his university.   No American poet ever had
smaller chances of reading in boyhood than Whittier.
Byrant was learned in comparison, his father being a
scholarly gentleman, with a good collection of books
which he encouraged his son in reading.   Scholarly
gentlemen also were the fathers of Longfellow and
Lowell, and able to give them the collegiate studies to
which they owed so much.   These gentlemen gave their
sons the education which the Quaker farmer of Haverhill
could not afford his son, and thus equipped they began
their literary career.   What their early verse was we know,
Longfellow's from the 'Voices of the Night,' in which he
included some of it, and Bryant's from the ordinary
edition of his poetical works, which after 'The Ages'
begins with 'Thanatopsis' written at seventeen or

thereabouts. . . . What Whittier's early verse is we know also, or may if we choose, by turning to the appendix of the fourth volume of the complete edition of his poetical works, where specimens of it are preserved. Dating from the age of eighteen onward, they are what might be expected from an uneducated country lad, from whom indifferent writing was not so much to be wondered at as any writing at all. Crude and feeble, imitative one might say, if one could detect any model that he had in view, conventional, experimental, tentative, its want of character may be inferred from some of its titles,— 'The Exile's Departure,' 'Deity,' 'Benevolence,' 'Ocean,' 'The Sicilian Vespers,' 'The Earthquake,' and so on. Such were Whittier's firstlings, of which he wrote when he was at last persuaded to collect them : ' That they met with some degree of favour at that time may be accounted for by the fact that the makers of verse were then few in number, with little competition in their unprofitable vocation, and that the standard of criticism was not discouragingly high.' "

" . . . Prominent among the literary beliefs of Whittier's boyhood was the delusion that an important element in American poetry existed in the lives of the aboriginal inhabitants of America, and that an American poet must needs celebrate the aborigines. Campbell shared it when he wrote his ' Gertrude of Wyoming,' an elegant but impossible poem ; and Bryant, Halleck, and Longfellow, shared it in their early years. It was the inspiration of Cooper, who evolved from his inner consciousness the ' noble savage ' of his ' Leather-stocking Tales,' and made his own name a household word the world over. That Whittier shared the delusion was natural, was inevitable one might say, it was so widely accepted ; and that it retarded rather than advanced his poetical pro- gress was also natural and inevitable. He did not discover this fact, however, until after he had written ' Mogg Megone,' 1834, and 'The Bridal of Pennacook,' 1844, two pieces of abortive narrative verse for which he soon ceased to care, and of the first of which he wrote in his later life : ' Looking at it at the present time, it suggests the idea of a big Indian in his war-paint strut- ting about in Sir Walter Scott's plaid.'

" . . . That, writing at all, he would write religious verse, might have been predicted from the reading to which he was chiefly restricted in his youth ; and that, continuing to write, he would write anti- slavery verse, might have been predicted from his ancestry. It was in his Quaker blood to hate every kind of oppression ; and of all the kinds with which he was acquainted, the meanest in those who practised it, as well as the most disgraceful in those who allowed it, was slavery. It was the greatest wrong that could be inflicted on the black race, and the greatest sin that could be committed by the white race, and it must be abolished. Impelled by these convictions, which were as much a part of his manhood as his religion, he cast his lot with the Abolitionists, sharing the obloquy which was cast upon them, and partaking their personal perils. To do this demanded more courage than was possessed by many worthy souls in New England, who, thinking as he did, concealed their thoughts and held their tongues and pens. He could do neither ; so he spoke what he thought and wrote what he felt, and very indignant writing it was. . . . That it was vigorous, more vigorous perhaps than anything of the kind in English speech, was as certain as that the impulse which created it was the imperative expression of the soul of Whittier as a man and a poet. As an American poet he had to write it, concerning as it did the country which he loved, and connected as it was with the history of human freedom. That it was not, except at intervals, poetical poetry, those of us who most clearly understand and most heartily admire his genius have to admit.

". . . Reading the poems of Whittier in the order in which they were written, we see that, while he blazed his path along the wilderness of contemporary politics, he suffered himself to loiter at times in one of the trails that connect the present with the past. It was not the dark and tangled trail where he had wandered in his bootless pursuit of the noble savage, but the golden trail that winds through our colonial history. He approached it in poems like 'Pentucket,' 'The Norsemen,' 'The Funeral Tree of the Sokokis'; he struck it in 'Cassandra Southwick,' 'The Exiles,' 'The New Wife and the Old.' He was the first poet to discover and explore the untrodden regions of American legendary lore, to restore its forgotten traditions to remembrance, and to illuminate with the light of his genius the dark backward and abysm of Time. His gifts were akin to those of the old English and Scotch balladists, who instinctively detected and seized the dramatic life of what they sang, and who, missing much that we now think poetical, never missed the hearts to which they addressed themselves, and which they touched and moved with pity and terror. What Whittier was slow in learning was that he was a natural balladist; but that fact, once learned, was never forgotten by him, though he was influenced by it at longer intervals than his readers wished. Running through the list of his narrative and legendary poems, we dwell upon those which we remember best, and which in most cases are ballads pure and simple, such, for instance, following their chronological arrangements, as 'Maud Muller,' 'The Garrison of Cape Ann,' 'Skipper Ireson's Ride,' 'The Swan Song of Parson Avery,' 'Cobbler Keezar's Vision,' 'John Underhill,' and 'Barbara Frietchie.' Closely related to these, in that their spirit is essentially that of balladry, are certain of his longer and more romantic poems, such as, to mention only a few, 'The Countess,' 'Among the Hills,' 'Marguerite,' 'The King's Missive,' 'The Bay of Seven Islands,' and 'How the Women went from Dover.'"

So writes Stoddard, noting the human element as stronger in Whittier than in any of his contemporaries. In the words of another critic, he has " done perhaps as much as all other poets put together to preserve the legends and immortalise the localities of the New England and Pennsylvanian portions of our country." And "in his treatment of legends his Quaker truthfulness comes in, and he produces his poetic effects while keeping close to history." He is true to the story as given to him, though the circumstances attached to the action of " Barbara Frietchie " are disputed; and though "poor old Floyd Ireson" bore really another name and was not so bad as the poet believed him to be. True to his country's past, shall we not also admire not only the true words, but the truthful life which sought to inspire his contemporaries and make them more worthy of poetic honour? Is he less a poet for drawing his inspiration from the present as well as the past? Would our greatest Shakespeare be less esteemed and reverenced if somewhere in his pages we found reference to the nobles and heroes of his own day?

CHAPTER XV.

SO early as 1864, in the pages of the *Atlantic Monthly*, Mr. David A. Wasson wrote a long, thoughtful study of Whittier, too long to be here given entire, but worth recalling in parts. Even for a lengthy quotation no apology need be offered, as it will help to complete our estimate of the New England poet.

"It was some ten years ago," writes Mr. Wasson, "that we first met John Greenleaf Whittier, the poet of the moral sentiment and of the heart and faith of the people of America. It chanced that we had then been making notes, with much interest, upon the genius of the Semitic nations. That peculiar simplicity, centrality, and intensity which caused them to originate Monotheism from two independent centres, the only systems of pure Monotheism which have had power in history—while the same characteristics made their poetry always lyrical, never epic or dramatic, and their most vigorous thought a perpetual sacrifice on the altars of the will—this had strongly impressed us; and we seemed to find in it a striking contrast to the characteristic genius of the Aryan or Indo-Germanic nations, with their imaginative interpretations of the religious sentiment, with their epic and dramatic expansions, and their taste for breadth and variety. Somewhat warm with these notions we came to a meeting with our poet, and the first thought on seeing him was—'The head of a Hebrew prophet!' It is not Hebrew—Saracen rather—the Jewish type is heavier, more material; but it corresponded strikingly to the conceptions we had formed of the Southern Semitic crania, and the whole make of the man was of the same character. The high cranium, so lofty especially in the dome—the slight and symmetrical backward slope of the whole head—the powerful level brows, and beneath these the dark, deep eyes, so full of shadowed fire—the Arabian complexion—the sharp-cut, intense lines of the face—the light, tall, erect stature—the quick axial poise of the movement—all these answered with singular accuracy to the picture of those preacher-races which had been shaping itself in our imagination. Indeed the impression was so strong as to induce some little feeling of embarrassment. It seemed slightly awkward and insipid to be meeting a prophet here in a parlour and in a spruce masquerade of modern costume, shaking hands, and saying 'Happy to meet you!' after the fashion of our feeble civilities.

" All this came vividly to remembrance on taking up, the other day, Whittier's last book of poems—' In War-time'—a volume that has been welcomed all over the land with enthusiastic delight. Had it been no more, however, than a mere personal reminiscence, it should, at present, have remained private. But have we not here a key to Whittier's genius? Is not this Semitic centrality and simplicity, this prophetic depth, reality, and vigour, without great lateral and intellectual range, its especial characteristic? He has not the liberated, light-winged Greek imagination — imagination not involved and included in the religious sentiment, but playing in epic freedom and with various interpretation between religion and intellect—ı.c has not the flowing, Protean, imaginative sympathy, the power of instant self-identification, with all forms of character and life which culminated in Shakespeare ; but that imaginative vitality which lurks in faith and conscience, producing what we may call *ideal force of heart*. This he has eminently ; and it is this central, invisible, Semitic heat which makes him a poet.

" Imagination exists in him, not as a separable faculty, but as a pure vital suffusion. Hence he is an *inevitable* poet. There is no drop of his blood, there is no fibre of his brain, which does not crave poetical expression. Mr. Carlyle desires to postpone poetry ; but, as Providence did not postpone Whittier, his wishes can hardly be gratified. Ours is indeed one of the plainest of poets. He is intelligible and acceptable to those who have little either of poetic culture or of fancy and imagination. Whoever has common sense and a sound heart has the powers by which he may be appreciated. And yet he is not only a real poet, but he is *all* poet. The Muses have not merely sprinkled his brow ; he was baptised by immersion. His notes are not many ; but in them Nature herself sings. He is a sparrow that half sings, half chirps, on a bush, not a lark that floods with orient hilarity the skies of the morning ; but the bush burns, like that which Moses saw, and the sparrow itself is part of the divine flame.

"This, then, is the general statement about Whittier. His genius is Hebrew, Biblical, more so than that of any other poet now using the English language. In other words, he is organically a poem of the Will. He is a flower of the moral sentiment, not in its flexible, feminine, vine-like dependence and play, but in its masculine vigour, climbing in direct, vertical affirmation, like a forest pine. In this respect he affiliates with Wordsworth and, going farther back, with Milton, whose tap-root was Hebrew, though in the vast epic flowering of his genius he passes beyond the imaginative range of the Semitic mind.

"In thus identifying our bard, spiritually, with a broad form of the genius of mankind we already say with emphasis that his is indeed a Life. Yes! once more a real Life. He is a nature. He was *born*, not manufactured. Here once again the old mysterious, miraculous processes of spiritual assimilation ! Here a genuine root-clutch upon the elements of man's experience, and an inevitable, indomitable working up of them into human shape ! To look at him without discerning this vital depth and reality were as good as no looking at all.

"Moreover the man and the poet are one and the same. His verse is no literary Beau-Brumelism, but a *re*presentation of that which is presented in his consciousness. First there is inward vital conversion of the elements of his experience, then verse, or version—first the soul, then the body. His voice, as such, has little range, nor is it any marvel of organic perfection ; on the contrary, there is many a voice with nothing at all in it which far surpasses his in mere vocal excellence; only in this you can hear the deep refrain of Nature, and of Nature chanting her moral ideal. . . .

"God gave Whittier a deep, hot, simple, strenuous, and yet ripe and spherical nature, whose twin necessities were, first, that it *must* lay an intense grasp on the elements of its experience; and, secondly, that it *must* work these up into some form of melodious completeness. History and the world gave him Quakerism, America, and rural solitude; and through this solitude went winding the sweet old Merrimac stream, the river that we would not wish to forget even by the waters of the river of life. And it is into these elements that his genius, with its peculiar vital simplicity and intensity, strikes root. Historic reality, the great *facts* of his time are the soil in which he grows, as they are with all natures of depth and energy. 'We did not wish,' said Goethe, 'to learn, but to live.'

"Quakerism and America (America ideally true to herself) quickly became in his mind one and the same. Quakerism means *divine democracy*. George Fox was the first forerunner, the John Baptist of the new time, leather-aproned in the British wilderness. Seeing the whole world dissolving into individualism, he did not try to tie it together, after the fashion of great old Hooker, with new cords of ecclesiasticism; but he did this—he affirmed a Mount Sinai in the heart of the individual, and gave to the word *person* an infinite depth. To sound that word was his function in history. No wonder that the English trembled with terror, and then blazed with rage. No wonder that many an ardent James Naylor was crazed with the new wine.

"Puritanism meant the same thing at bottom; but accepting the more legal and learned interpretations of Calvin, it was, to a great degree, involved in the past, and also turned its eye more to political mechanisms. For this very reason it kept up more of fellowship with the broad world, and had the benefit of this in a larger measure of social fructification. Whatever is separated dies. Quakerism uttered a word so profound that the utterance made it insular; and, left to itself, it began to be lost in itself. Nevertheless Quakerism and Puritanism are the two richest soils of modern time.

"Our young poet got at the heart of the matter. He learned to utter the word *Man* so believingly that it sounded down into depths of the divine and infinite. He learned to say, with Novalis, 'He touches heaven who touches a human body.' And when he uttered this word *Man* in full social breadth, lo! it changed and became *America*.

"There begins the genesis of the conscious poet. All the depths of his heart rang with the resonance of these imaginations—*Man*, *America*; meaning divine depth of manhood, divine spontaneity and rectitude of social relationship.

"But what, what is this? Just as he would raise his voice to chant the new destinies of man, a harsh, heartless, human bark, and therewith a low, despairing stifle of sobbing, came to his ear. It is the bark of the auctioneer, 'Going! going!'—it is the sobbing of the slave on the auction block. And *this*, too, O Poet! this, too, is America. So you are not secure of your grand believing imaginations yet; but must fight for them. The faith of your heart would perish if it did not put on armour.

". . . The faith for which he fought is uttered with spirit in a stanza from the ' Branded Hand ' :—

> ' In thy lone and long night watches,
>   sky above and wave below,
> Thou didst learn a higher wisdom
>   than the babbling schoolmen know :.
> God's stars and silence taught thee,
>   as His angels only can,
> That the one sole sacred thing
>   beneath the cope of heaven is Man !'

Did he not choose as a poet *must?* Between a low moral prosaicism and generous moral ideal was it possible for him to hesitate ? Are there those whose real thought is that man, beyond his estimation as an animal, represents only a civil value—that he is but the tailor's ' dummy ' and clothes-horse of institutions ? Do they tell our poet that his notion of man as a divine revelation, as a pure spiritual or absolute value, is a mere dream, discountenanced by the truth of the universe ? He might answer, ' Let the universe look to it then ! In that case I stand upon my dream as the only worthy reality.' What were a mere pot-and-pudding universe to him ? Does Mr. Holyoake [1] complain that

---

[1] An English objector who had complained of the impolitic violence of Garrison and his fellow Abolitionists.

these hot idealisms make the culinary kettles of the world boil over? Kitchen prudences are good for kitchens; but the sun kindles his great heart without special regard to them.

"These 'Voices of Freedom' are no bad reading at the present day. They are of that strenuous quality that the light of battle brings to view a finer point which lay unseen between the lines. They are themselves battles, and stir the blood like the blast of a trumpet. What a heat in them of fiery pulses! What a heat as of molten metal, or coal mines burning underground! What anger! What desire! And yet we have in vain searched these poems to find one trace of base wrath or of any degenerate and selfish passion. He is angry, and sins not. The sun goes down and again rises upon his wrath; and neither sets nor rises upon aught freer from meanness and egoism. All the fires of his heart burn for justice and mercy, for God and Humanity; and they who are most scathed by them owe him no hatred in return, whether they pay him any or not.

". . . These voices are less to be named poems than pieces of rhythmic oratory, oratory crystallised into poetic form, and carrying that deeper significance and force which from all vitalised form are inseparable. A poem, every work of art, must rest in itself; oratory is a means toward a specific effect. The man who writes poems may have aims which underlie and suffuse his work; but they must not be partial, they must be co-extensive with the whole spirit of man, and must enter his work as the air enters his nostrils. The moment a definite partial effect is sought, the attitude of poetry begins to be lost. These battle-pieces are, therefore, a warfare for the possession of the poet's ideal, not the joyous life-breath of that ideal already victorious in him. And the other poems of this first great epoch in his poetical life, though always powerful, often beautiful, yet never, we think, show a perfect resting upon his own poetic heart.

" . . . Yet they are sterling poems, with the stamp of the mint upon them. And some of the strains are such as no living man but Whittier has proven his power to produce. 'Ichabod,' for example, is the purest and pro-foundest *moral* lament, to the best of our knowledge, in modern literature, whether American or European. It is the grief of angels in arms over a traitor brother slain on the battlefields of heaven."

So much, not too much, from a competent and care-ful student of the poet's work, may help us to know what he was; but to know him thoroughly we must read and weigh the whole product of his muse, and so learn what were the impulses that from time to time stirred him to expression, so trace his poetic growth through the course of many years. A few more of Mr. Wasson's well-said words may be farther aid to our appreciation.

"It is in his ballads that Whittier exhibits, not per-haps a higher, yet a rarer power than elsewhere, a power in truth, which is very rare indeed. . . . He has developed of late years the precious power of creating *homely beauty*, one of the rarest powers shown in modern literature. Homely life-scenes, homely old sanctities and heroisms, he takes up, delineates them with intrepid fidelity in their homeliness, and lo ! there they are, beautiful as Indian corn, or as ploughed land under an October sun.

". . . 'Skipper Ireton's Ride,'—can any one tell what makes that poetry? This uncertainty is the highest praise. This power of telling a plain matter in a plain way, and leaving it there a symbol and harmony for ever, is the power of Nature herself. And again we repeat, that almost anything may be found in literature more frequently than this pure creative simplicity."

And again—"Whittier's landscape pictures alone make his books worthy of study."

But we may turn now to another of those who have known him and made a careful study of his writings, to Mr. Stedman, already referred to, "poet and friend of poets," to whom Whittier's last publication was dedi-cated. From a long paper in his "Poets of America" (1885), we may gather into closer shape the scattered frag-ments of the story already given. With it we may close biography and criticism, adding only the briefest sum-ming up of both.

"Whittier's origin and early life," writes Stedman, "were auspicious for one who was to become a poet of the people. His muse shielded him from the relaxing influence of luxury and superfine culture. These could not reach the primitive homestead in the beautiful Merrimac Valley, five miles out from the market-town of Haverhill, where all things were elementary and of the plainest cast. The training of the Friends made his boyhood more simple, otherwise it mattered little whether he derived from Puritan or Quaker sources. Still it was much, in one respect, to be descended from

Quakers and Huguenots used to suffer and be strong for conscience' sake. It placed him years in advance of the comfortable Brahmin class, with its blunted sense of right and wrong, and, to use his own words, turned him 'so early away from what Roger Williams calls the world's great trinity, pleasure, profit, and honour, to take side with the poor and oppressed.' . . . Whittier's Quaker strain yielded him wholly to the 'intellectual passion.' That transcendentalism aroused, and still keeps him obedient to the Inward Light. And it made him a poet militant, a crusader, whose moral weapons, since he must disown the carnal, were keen of edge and seldom in their scabbards. The fire of his deep-set eyes, whether betokening, like that of his kinsman Webster, the Batchelder blood, or inherited from some old Feuillevert, strangely contrasts with the benign expression of his mouth,—that firm serenity which by transmitted habitude dwells upon the lips of the sons and daughters of peace.

"There was no affectation in the rusticity of his youth. It was the real thing, the neat and saving homeliness of the eastern farm. . . . Of our leading poets he was almost the only one who learned Nature by working with her at all seasons, under the sky and in the wood and field. So much for his boyhood. . . . From that time we see the poet working upward in the old-fashioned way. A clever youth need not turn gauger in a land of schools and newspapers. Whittier's training was supplemented by a year or more at the Academy, and by a winter's practice as a teacher himself—fulfilling thus the customary *Lehr-jahre* of our village aspirants.

In another year we find him the conductor of a tariff newspaper in Boston. Before his twenty-fifth birthday he had experienced the vicissitudes of old-time journalism, changing from one desk to another, at Haverhill, Boston, and Hartford, still pursuing literature, ere long known as a poet and sketch-writer, and near the close of this period issuing his first book, of ' Legends ' in prose and verse.

" . . . But the mission of his life now came upon him. . . . Garrison's crusade was one to which his whole nature inclined him. It was no personal ambition that made him the psalmist of the new movement. His verses, crude as they were, had gained favour; he already had a name, and a career was predicted for him. He now doomed himself to years of retardation and disfavour, and had no reason to foresee the honours they would bring him in the end. What he tells us is the truth : ' For twenty years my name would have injured the circulation of any of the literary or political journals in the country.' . . . Bryant, many years later, pointed out that in recent times the road of others to literary success had been made smooth by anti-slavery opinions, adding that in Whittier's case the reverse of that was true; that he made himself the champion of the slave ' when to say aught against the national curse was to draw upon one's self the bitterest hatred, loathing, and contempt, of the great majority of men throughout the land.' Unquestionably Whittier's ambition, during his novitiate, had been to do something as a poet and a man of letters. Not that he had learned what few in fact at that time realised, that the highest art aims at creative beauty, and that devotion, repose, and calm, are essential to the mastery of an ideal. . . . We measure poetry at its worth, not at the worth of the maker. This is the law; yet in Whittier's record, if ever, there is an appeal to the higher law that takes note of exceptions. Some of his verse, as a pattern for verse hereafter, is not what it might have been if he had consecrated himself to poetry as an art; but it is memorably connected with historic times, and his rudest shafts of song were shot true and far and tipped with flame. . . . His songs touched the hearts of his people. It was the generation which listened in childhood to the ' Voices of Freedom,' that fulfilled their prophecies.

". . . Soon he was writing abolition pamphlets, editing the *Freeman*, and active in the thick of the conflict. He was the secretary of the first anti-slavery convention, a signer of the Declaration of Sentiments, and, at an age when bardlings are making sonnets to a mistress's eyebrow, he was facing mobs at Plymouth, Boston, Philadelphia. After seven or eight years of this stormy service he settled down in quarters at Amesbury, sending out, as ever, his prose and verse to forward the cause. But now his humane and fervent motives were understood even by opponents, and the sweetness of his rural lyrics and idylls had testified for him as a poet. The most eclectic of publishing houses welcomed him to its list; the rise of poetry had set in, and Longfellow, Emerson, Lowell, were gaining a constituency. As he grew in favour, attractive editions of his poems appeared, and his later volumes came from the press as frequently as Longfellow's,—more than one of them, like ' Snowbound,' receiving in this country as warm and wide a welcome as those of the Cambridge Laureate. After the war Garrison, at last crowned with honour and rejoicing in the consummation of his work, was seldom heard. Whittier in his hermitage, the resort of many pilgrims, has steadily renewed his song. While chanting in behalf of every patriotic or humane effort of his time, he has been the truest singer of our homestead and wayside life, and has rendered all the legends of his region into familiar, verse. The habit of youth has clung to him, and he often misses, in his too facile rhyme and rhythm, the graces, the studied excellence of modern work. But all in all, as we have seen, and more than others, he has read the heart of New England.

". . . It would not be fair to test Whittier by the quality of his off-hand work. His verse always was auxiliary to what he deemed the main business of his life, and has varied with the occasions that inspired it. His object was not the artist's, to make the occasion serve his poem, but directly the reverse. . . . Probably it occurred somewhat late to the mind of that pure and duteous enthusiast that there is such a thing as duty to one's art. . . . Nor is it strange that the artistic moral sense of a Quaker poet, reared on a New England farmstead, at first should be deficient. . . . His ear and voice were naturally fine, as some of his early work plainly shows, ' Cassandra Southwick ' for instance. . . . If he had occupied himself wholly with poetic work, he would have grown as steadily as his most successful compeers. But his vocation became that of trumpeter to the impetuous reform brigade. He supplied verse on the instant, often full of vigour, but often little more than the rallying blast of a passing campaign. We are told that from 1832 to the close of our dreadful war in 1865 'his harp of liberty was never hung up.' Not an important occasion escaped him.

". . . His imperfections were those of his time and class. He never learned compression, and still [1885] is troubled more with fatal fluency than our other poets of equal rank,—by an inability to reject poor stanzas and to stop at the right place. But there came a period when his verse was composed with poetic intent and after a less careless fashion. . . . His first ballads give the clew to his genius, and now make it apparent that most of his verse may be considered without much regard to dates of production. 'Cassandra Southwick,' alone, showed where his strength lay ; of all our poets he is the most natural balladist. . . . His Quaker strains, chanted while the sect is slowly blending with the world's people, seem like its death song. . . . And as a bucolic poet of his own section, rendering its pastoral life and aspect, Whittier surpasses all rivals. . . . Long-fellow's rural pieces were done by a skilled workman, who could regard his themes objectively and put them to good use. Lowell delights in out-door life, and his Yankee studies are perfect ; still we feel that he is intellectually and socially miles above the people of the vales. Whittier is of their blood, and always the boy-poet of the Essex farm, however advanced in years and fame. They are won by the sincerity and ingenuous-ness of his verse, rooted in the soil and nature as the fern and wild-rose of the wayside. . . . He himself despises a sham pastoral. There is good criticism, a clear sense of what is needed, in his paper on Robert Dinsmore, the old Scotch bard of his childhood. He says of rural poetry that 'the mere dilettante and the amateur ruralist may as well keep their hands off. The prize is not for them. He who would successfully strive for it must be himself what he sings, one who has added to his book-lore the large experience of an active partici- pation in the rugged toil, the hearty amusements, the trials and pleasures he describes.'"

Enough of criticism, even the most appreciative, and only the appreciative can be just. All said, we may divide his work into rhetorical and purely artistic poetry. Much was uttered in eager, unfinished, not-much-con- sidered verse, because strongly felt, and fashioned from the feelings with one single object, to stir the hearts of others, not in any sense put forth as exercises in rhyme, exploits for the world's admiration or in search of poetic fame. Allow that this carelessness detracts from all verse so put forth, enough yet remains of Whittier's more artistic work to place him in the glorious company of the best of his poet contemporaries; and, passing all literary judgment, he is to be remembered and honoured as a poet who never forgot the duty or the dignity of a man : his

> " Life made by duty epical,
>   And rhythmic with the truth."

INDEX.

------◆◆------

A.

American Manufacturer, Whittier edits, 58

American Monthly Magazine, formerly *New England Magazine,* 89 ; Whittier's contributions to, 90

Amesbury, 22, 25, 41 ; family moves to, 77, 115, 163

Anti-Slavery Standard, Whittier writes for, 79, 108

Atlantic Monthly, Whittier writes for, 63, 101, 108 ; Whittier aids in organising, 124, 125, 141, 183

"At Sundown," 160

B.

"Barefoot Boy," quoted, 45-47

Boston Pearl, Whittier writes for, 91

Brainard, J. J. C., his poems edited by Whittier, 59

"Branded Hand," quoted, 189

Brown, John, the Abolitionist hero, settles in Kansas, 129, 130 ; fights pro-slavery raiders from Missouri, 130 ; description and character of, 130, 131 ; obtains possession of armoury at Harper's Ferry, 131 ; cannot hold it, taken prisoner, 132 ; Whittier's praise of, 132-134

Burns, Whittier's introduction to poems of, 49, 84, 171, 177

C.

"Cassandra Southwick," 91 ; quoted, 92-94, 196, 197

Coates, Lindley, the Abolitionist, 65

Coffin, Joshua, poet's first schoolmaster, 43, 49, 66

"Complete Poems," 112, 114

D.

Democratic Review, Whittier writes for, 91

"Dream of Summer," quoted, 175-176

E.

Emancipator, Whittier writes for, 79, 91, 108

Emerson, 12, 125, 195

F.

Free Press, 50, 57

G.

Garrison, Lloyd, edits *Free Press,* 50 ; edits *National Philanthropist,* 57, 58 ; edits *Liberator,* 61 ; his influence on Whittier, 62, 63, 65, 68, 123, 125, 138, 194, 196

Greeley, Horace, 14

Greenleaf, Sarah, poet's grandmother, 17 ; her ancestry, 18

Greenleaf, Simon, poet's relation, 19

H.

Hartford, Whittier at, 58, 89, 194

Haverhill, 21, 26 ; Academy at, 53, 57, 62, 67, 73, 77, 89, 163, 194

Haverhill Gazette, poet writes for, 53, 57 ; edits, 58, 79, 91

"Hazel Blossoms," 150

"Henchman," quoted, 153, 154

"Hero," 115 ; quoted, 116–118

"Home Ballads, Poems, and Lyrics," 127

Howe, Dr. Samuel G., described by Whittier, 115–118

I.

"Ichabod," quoted, 106, 107, 191

"In School Days," 143 ; quoted, 144, 145

"In War Time," 184

J.

"Justice and Expediency," &c., Abolition pamphlet by Whittier, 62

K.

Kennedy, Mr., poet's biographer, 21, 24, 49, 77

L.

"Laus Deo," quoted, 142

"Lays of my Home and other Poems," 91

"Letters of John Quincy Adams to his constituents," edited by Whittier, 74

Liberator, Whittier writes for, 79, 91, 108

"Literary Recreations," 110, 114

Livermore, Harriet, pilgrim preacher, character described by Whittier, 39-42

Longfellow, 12, 125, 165, 177, 178, 195, 197

Lowell, 22, 78, 115

Lowell, James Russell, 12, 68, 90, 125, 165, 177, 195, 197

M.

"Margaret Smith's Journal," 111, 112

May, Samuel T., the Abolitionist, 65, 67

"Memories," quoted, 95, 96

Merrimac, Valley of, poet's home, 16, 21-29, 66, 97–99, 192

Middlesex Standard, Whittier writes for, 78

Milton, 15, 60, 70–72, 140

"Mogg Megone," 74, 90

"Moll Pitcher," 89

Mott, Lucretia, 63

Mussey, B. B., Whittier's publisher, 113

"My Summer with Dr. Singletary," 96, 97

National Era, Whittier writes for, 79 ; edits, 101, 108, 114, 115, 118

N.
" New England Legends," 59

New England Review, Whittier edits, 58, 59

New York Mirror, Whittier writes for, 91

O.
Oak Noll, home of Whittier's latter years, 77

P.
Parkman, Mr., calls Whittier Poet of New England, 11, 12

" Pastoral Letter," quoted, 82–85

Pennsylvania Freeman, Whittier edits, 74 ; offices burnt, 75, 76, 77, 195

" Pennsylvania Pilgrim," 145–147

Philadelphia Anti-Slavery Convention, 63 ; Whittier's description of, 65, 66

" Pine Tree," quoted, 87

Pitman, Mrs. Harriet, describes Whittier as a young man, 54–57

Plummer, Jonathan, Yankee troubadour, 47, 48

Poe, Edgar Allan, compared with Whittier, 170, 171

" Poems written during the progress of the Abolition Question in the United States," 74

" Portraits," 109

S.
" Sea Dream," quoted, 150, 151

Shipley, Thomas, the Abolitionist, 66

" Shoemaker," quoted, 114

" Singer, the," 147

" Skipper Ireton's Ride," 192

" Snowbound," quoted, 30, 33–41, 42, 167, 176, 195

" Songs of Labour," 114

" Songs of Three Centuries," compiled by Whittier, 159, 160

Stanton, Henry B., friend of Whittier, 78

" Stanzas," quoted, 80

Stedman, Mr., on Whittier, 11, 12–15, 164, 192–198

Stoddard, Richard Henry, on Whittier, 174, 176, 181

" Stranger in Lowell," 78

" Sunset," quoted, 155–157

T.
" Telling the Bees," quoted, 171–173

" Tent on the Beach," 140, 141, 142

Thayer family, poet boards with, 53

" The Meeting," quoted, 121

" The Sisters," quoted, 147–150

Thompson, George, the Abolitionist, 68

" To Oliver Wendell Holmes," quoted, 162

U.
Underwood, Mr., Whittier's biographer, 79, 84, 85, 89

V.
" Vaudois Teacher," 58

" Views of Slavery and Emancipation," edited by Whittier, 74

" Vision of Echard," quoted, 154

"Voices of Freedom," 79, 80, 81–85, 86–88, 91, 92 121, 123, 153, 166, 190, 191

W.

Wasson, David A., his study on Whittier, 183–192

Whittier, Abigail (*née* Hussey), poet's mother, 17 ; portrait, 21, 56 ; character, 31–34, 77 ; death, 115

Whittier, Elizabeth, poet's favourite sister, 17 ; character, 36, 56, 57, 77, 112, 115 ; her poems, 151

Whittier, John, poet's father, 17, 25 ; character, 30, 56 ; death, 58

Whittier, John Greenleaf, claim to the title of Poet of New England, 11–15 ; Birth, 17, 18, 27, 29 ; boyhood, 43–52 ; publishes first poem, 50 ; character as a young man, 53–56 ; goes to Haverhill Academy, 53 ; goes to Boston, 58 ; returns home, 58 ; goes to Hartford, 58 ; publishes " New England Legends," 59 ; becomes secretary of Philadelphia Anti-slavery Convention, 63 ; describes members of Convention, 65, 66 ; explains his taking part, though a Quaker, in Abolition strife, 69–72 ; elected member for Haverhill, in State Legislature, 73 ; political character, 73 ; publishes " Mogg Megone," 74 ; edits " Letters of John Quincy Adams to his Constituents," 74 ; " Views of Slavery and Emancipation," 74 ; " Poems written during the progress of the Abolition Question in the United States," 74 ; goes to Pennsylvania, 74 ; edits *Pennsylvania Freeman*, 74 ; returns to Haverhill, 77 ; goes to Amesbury, 77 ; writes for *Middlesex Standard*, 78 ; " The Stranger in Lowell," 78 ; writes " Pastoral Letter," 81 ; writes for *Democratic Review*, 91 ; edits *National Era*, 101 ; writes " Portraits," 109 ; " Literary Recreations," 110 ; " Margaret Smith's Journal," 111, 112 ; aids in organising *Atlantic Monthly*, 124, 125 ; attitude during the war, 132–139 ; devotes himself to his art, 140-162 ; dies, 163 ; funeral, 163, 164 ; his legacies, 165 ; criticism of Whittier as a poet, 166–193 ; Mr. Wasson's general description of his personal appearance, 184 ; review of life, 193–198

Whittier, Mary, poet's sister, 17 ; character, 36, 115

Whittier, Matthew, poet's brother, 17, 115

Whittier, Moses, poet's uncle, 25 ; character, 34, 35, 45, 50, 115

Whittier, Thomas, ancestor of poet, 16 ; emigration to, and life in America, 16, 17 ; builds house in which poet was born, 26

Whitsun, Thomas, the Abolitionist, 66

Wordsworth, compared with Whittier, 171

BIBLIOGRAPHY.

BY

JOHN P. ANDERSON

(*British Museum*).

I. COLLECTED WORKS.

II. SEPARATE WORKS.

III. SELECTIONS.

IV. APPENDIX—
Biography, Criticism, etc.
Magazine Articles, etc.

V. CHRONOLOGICAL LIST OF WORKS.

I. COLLECTED WORKS.

The Writings of John Greenleaf Whittier. Riverside edition. 7 vols. Boston, 1888-89, 8vo.

The Writings of John Greenleaf Whittier. 7 vols. London, 1888-89, 8vo.

Miscellaneous Poems. Boston, 1844, 8vo.

Ballads and other poems. [With a preface by E. Wright.] London, 1844, 16mo.

Poems. Illustrated by H. Billings. Boston, 1849, 8vo.

——Another edition. Boston, 1850, 8vo.

——Another edition. Boston, 1856, 8vo.

Poetical Works. London, 1850, 24mo.

The Poetical Works of John Greenleaf Whittier. 2 vols. Boston, 1857, 16mo.

——Another edition. Boston, 1867, 12mo.

——Another edition, with illustrations. Boston, 1869, 12mo.

——Poems. New revised edition. With thirty-two illustrations. Boston, 1874, 8vo.

——Another edition. The Complete Poetical Works of John Greenleaf Whittier. Household edition. Boston, 1874, 8vo.

——Another edition. London, 1874, 16mo.

The Complete Poetical Works of John Greenleaf Whittier. With numerous illustrations. Boston, 1876, 8vo.

——Another edition. 3 vols. Boston, 1880. 8vo.

——Another edition. With critical biography by W. M. Rossetti. London [1880], 8vo.
  Forms part of " Moxon's Popular Poets."
——Another edition. With numerous illustrations. London [1881], 8vo.
The Poetical Works of John Greenleaf Whittier. With a prefatory notice by Eva Hope. London, 1885, 8vo.
  Vol. of " The Canterbury Poets."
The Poetical Works of John Greenleaf Whittier. A new edition. London, 1890, 8vo.
The Poetical Works of John Greenleaf Whittier. With life, notes, index, etc. London, 1891, 8vo.
  The " Albion " edition.

Prose Works of John Greenleaf Whittier. 2 vols. Boston, 1866, 8vo.

II. SEPARATE WORKS.

Legends of New England. [Prose and Verse.] Hartford, 1831, 8vo.
Moll Pitcher. Boston, 1832, 16mo.
——Moll Pitcher, and the Minstrel Girl. Poems. Revised edition. Philadelphia, 1840, 16mo.
The Literary Remains of John G. C. Brainard, with a sketch of his life. Hartford [1832], 12mo.
Justice and Expediency ; or, Slavery considered with a View to its Rightful and Effectual Remedy, Abolition. Haverhill, 1833, 8vo.
Mogg Megone. A poem. Boston, 1836, 32mo.
Views of Slavery and Emancipation ; from " Society in America," by Harriet Martineau. [Edited.] New York, 1837, 16mo.

Letters from John Quincey Adams to his Constituents of the Twelfth Congressional District in Massachusetts. [With a preface and two poems against slavery, by J. G. Whittier.] Boston, 1837, 8vo.
Poems written during the Progress of the Abolition Question in the United States between the years 1830 and 1838. Boston, 1837, 16mo.
Ballads, Anti-Slavery, etc. Philadelphia, 1838, 16mo.
The North Star : The Poetry of Freedom by her Friends. [Edited.] Philadelphia, 1840, 8vo.
Lays of my Home, and other poems. Boston, 1843, 12mo.
The Stranger in Lowell. Boston, 1845, 12mo.
  Appeared originally in the *Middlesex Standard.*
Voices of Freedom. Fifth edition. Philadelphia, 1846, 8vo.
——Another edition. Philadelphia, 1849, 8vo.
The Supernaturalism of New England. London, 1847, 12mo.
  Part of " Wiley and Putnam's Library of American Books."
Leaves from Margaret Smith's Journal. Boston, 1849, 16mo.
Songs of Labor, and other poems. Boston, 1850, 12mo.
  Originally appeared in the *Democratic Review* and the *National Era.*
Old Portraits and Modern Sketches. Boston, 1850, 8vo.
  Appeared originally in the *National Era.*
Little Eva ; Uncle Tom's Guardian Angel. Boston, 1852, 4to.
  Consists of 4 pp. Music by Emilio Manuel.
The Chapel of the Hermits, and

other poems. Boston, 1853, 12mo.
Appeared originally in the *National Era.*

A Sabbath Scene. [A poem.] Illustrations by Baker, Smith, and Andrew. Boston, 1853, 8vo.
Published by Ticknor, Reed, & Fields. An edition was brought out the following year by John P. Jewett & Co., of Boston.

Literary Recreations and Miscellanies. Boston, 1854, 8vo.
Appeared originally in the *National Era.*

The Panorama, and other poems. Boston, 1856, 8vo.

Home Ballads, Poems, and Lyrics. Boston, 1860, 8vo.

In War Time, and other poems. Boston, 1863, 8vo.

The Patience of Hope. [By Dora Greenwell]. With an introduction by John G. Whittier. Boston, 1863, 8vo.

Snow-Bound. A winter idyl. Boston, 1866, 8vo.

——Another edition. London, 1867, 8vo.

——Another edition. With illustrations. Boston, 1868, 8vo.

——Another edition. Illustrated. Boston, 1875, 24mo.
Part of the " Vest-Pocket Series of Standard and Popular Authors."

——Another edition. With explanatory notes. Boston, 1883, 8vo.
No. 4 of " The Riverside Literature Series."

——Another edition. With designs by E. H. Garrett. London, 1891, 8vo.

Maud Muller. [A poem.] With illustrations by W. J. Hennessy. Boston, 1867, 8vo.
Re-issued in 1872. Appeared originally in the *National Era,* 1854.

——Another edition. With illustrations by G. Carline. London [1886], 4to.

——Another edition. London [1891], 16mo.

National Lyrics. Illustrated by W. J. Hennessy. Boston, 1867, 16mo.
The third of the Series of "Companion Poets for the People."

The Tent on the Beach, and other poems. Boston, 1867, 8vo.

——Another edition. Illustrated. Boston, 1877, 24mo.
Part of the " Vest-Pocket Series of Standard and Popular Authors."

Among the Hills, and other poems. Boston, 1869, 8vo.

Ballads of New England. With illustrations [from sketches by Harry Fenn]. Boston, 1870, 8vo.

Two Letters on the present aspect of the Society of Friends. Reprinted from the Philadelphia *Friends' Review.* London, 1870, 8vo.

Miriam, and other poems. Boston, 1871, 8vo.

Child Life : a collection of poems. Edited by John Greenleaf Whittier. With illustrations. Boston, 1872 [1871], 8vo.

——Another edition. Boston, 1873, 8mo.

——Another edition. London, 1874, 8vo.

The Pennsylvania Pilgrim, and other poems. Boston, 1872, 16mo.
A copy in the British Museum is dated 1873.

The Journal of John Woolman. With an introduction by John G. Whittier. Boston, 1872, 8vo.

Child Life in prose. Edited by John Greenleaf Whittier. Illustrated. Boston, 1874, 8vo.

——Another edition. London, [1880], 8vo.

Mabel Martin, and other poems. With notes and a biographical sketch. Boston, 1884, 16mo.
No. 5 of the "Riverside Literature Series." Mabel Martin is an amplification of "The Witch's Daughter."

——Another edition, with illustrations. Boston, 1876, 16mo.

Hazel-Blossoms. (Poems.) Boston, 1875, 8vo.

Songs of Three Centuries. [An Anthology.] Edited by J. G. Whittier. Boston, 1876, 8vo.

——New revised edition. With illustrations. Boston, 1877, 8vo.

The Vision of Echard, and other poems. Boston, 1878, 8vo.

William Lloyd Garrison, and his times. With an introduction by J. G. Whittier. Boston, 1880, 8vo.

The River Path. Boston, 1880, 8vo.
One of the four poems in *Christmastide*, etc.

The King's Missive, and other poems. Boston, 1881, 8vo.
Appeared originally in *The Memorial History of Boston*, vol. i. pp. xxv.-xxxii.

——The King's Missive, Mabel Martin, and later poems. London, 1881, 12mo.

Letters of Lydia Maria Child. With a biographical introduction by John G. Whittier, and an appendix by Wendell Phillips. Boston, 1883, 8vo.

The Bay of Seven Islands, and other poems. Boston, 1883, 8vo.

——Another edition. London, 1883, 8vo.

Poems of Nature. Illustrated from nature by E. Kingsley. Boston, 1886, 4to.

Saint Gregory's Guest, and recent poems. Boston, 1886, 8vo.

American Literature, and other papers by Edwin Percy Whipple. With introductory note by J. G. Whittier. Boston, 1887, 8vo.

At Sundown. [Poems]. With designs by E. H. Garrett. Riverside Press: Cambridge, 1892, 8vo.
An edition of this volume was privately printed in 1890.

III. SELECTIONS.

Poems on Slavery by Longfellow, Whittier, Southey, H. B. Stowe, etc. London, 1853, 8vo.
The poems by Whittier are chiefly taken from the "Poems written during the progress of the Abolition Question."

Favorite Poems. Illustrated. Boston, 1877, 12mo.

American Prose: Hawthorne, Irving, Longfellow, Whittier, Holmes, etc. Boston, 1880, 8vo.
Contains two pieces by Whittier—the "Yankee Gypsies" and "The Boy Captives."

The Whittier Birthday Book. Arranged by Elizabeth S. Owen. Boston, 1881, 16mo.

Leaflets from Standard Authors. Whittier. Poems and prose passages from the works of J. G. Whittier. Compiled by Josephine E. Hodgdon. Boston, 1882, 8vo.

Text and verse for every day in the year. Scripture passages and parallel selections from the writings of John G. Whittier. Arranged by Gertrude W. Cartland. London, 1885, 16mo.

Birthday Chimes from Whittier. Selections from the poems of J. G. Whittier. By J. R. E. P. Edinburgh [1892], 16mo.

IV. APPENDIX.

BIOGRAPHY, CRITICISM, ETC.

Bartlett, David W. — Modern Agitators: or pen portraits of living American Reformers. New York, 1856, 8vo.
John Greenleaf Whittier, pp. 240-265.

Bungay, George W.—Off-Hand Takings ; or, Crayon Sketches of the noticeable men of our age. New York [1860], 8vo.
John Greenleaf Whittier, pp. 132-140.

Chase, George W.—The History of Haverhill. Haverhill, 1861, 8vo.
Numerous references to Whittier.

Duyckinck, George L.--The Cyclopædia of American Literature, etc. 2 vols. Philadelphia, 1877, 8vo.
Whittier, vol. ii., pp. 312-319.

Grimke, A. H. — William Lloyd Garrison, the Abolitionist. New York, 1891, 8vo.
Numerous references to Whittier.

Griswold, Rufus W.—The Poets and Poetry of America. Philadelphia, 1856, 8vo.
Whittier, pp. 389-406.

Hamilton, Walter.—Parodies of the Works of English and American Authors, etc. London, 1888, 8vo.
J. G. Whittier, vol. v., pp. 239-245.

Hazeltine, Mayo Williamson.— Chats about Books, Poets, and Novelists. New York, 1883, 8vo.
Whittier, pp. 212-226.

Kennedy, W. Sloane. — John Greenleaf Whittier, his life, genius, and writings. Boston, 1882, 8vo.

——John G. Whittier, the Poet of Freedom.—New York, 1892, 8vo.
Part of the "American Reformers' series.

Lowell, James Russell.—A Fable for Critics. London, 1892, 8vo.
Whittier, pp. 58-61.

Massachusetts Historical Society. —Proceedings of the Massachusetts Historical Society. Boston, 1881, 8vo.
A Paper read by the Rev. Dr. Ellis on "The King's Missive," vol. xviii., 1881, pp. 357-362; Whittier's Reply, pp. 387-394; Dr. Ellis's Answer, pp. 394-399.

May, Samuel J.—Some recollections of our Anti-Slavery Conflict. Boston, 1869, 8vo.
John G. Whittier and the Anti-Slavery Poets, pp. 259-266.

Mitford, Mary Russell.—Recollections of a literary life. New edition. London, 1859, 8vo.
John Greenleaf Whittier, pp. 309-314.

Parton, James. — Some noted princes, authors, and statesmen, etc. New York [1886], 8vo.
The Home of J. G. Whittier, by H. Butterworth, pp. 219-323.

Richardson, Charles F.—American Literature, 1607-1885. New York, 1891, 8vo.
Numerous references to Whittier.

Sargent, Mrs. John T.—Sketches and Reminiscences of the Radical Club of Chestnut Street, Boston. Boston, 1880, 8vo.
Contains poems and letters by Whittier, and a description of his meeting with the Emperor of Brazil, Dom Pedro.

Shepard, William.—Pen Pictures of Modern Authors. New York, 1882, 8vo.
Longfellow and Whittier, pp. 119-134.

Stedman, Edmund C.—Poets of America. Boston, 1885, 8vo.
Numerous references to Whittier.

Taylor, Bayard.—Critical Essays and Literary Notes. New York, 1880, 8vo.

John Greenleaf Whittier, pp. 294-296.

——Life and Letters of Bayard Taylor. 2 vols. Boston, 1884, 8vo.

Numerous references to Whittier.

Underwood, Francis H. — John Greenleaf Whittier ; a biography. London, 1884, 8vo.

Whipple, Edwin P. — American Literature and other Papers. Boston, 1887, 8vo.

Whittier, pp. 73-76.

Whittier, Charles Collyer.—Genealogy of the Whittier Family, 1622-1882. Boston, 1882, s. sh. fol.

Printed for private distribution.

Whittier, John Greenleaf.—Proceedings at a presentation of a portrait of John Greenleaf Whittier to Friends' School, Providence, R. I., 1884. Cambridge, 1885, 8vo.

Wilson, James Grant, and Fiske, John.—Appleton's Cyclopædia of American Biography. New York, 1889, 8vo.

J. G. Whittier, vol. vi. (with portrait), pp. 493, 494.

Winks, William Edward.—Lives of Illustrious Shoemakers. London, 1883, 8vo.

J. G. Whittier, "the Quaker poet," pp. 364-369.

MAGAZINE ARTICLES, Etc.

Whittier, John Greenleaf. North American Review, by E. P. Whipple, vol. 58, 1844, pp. 30-32.—Irish Quarterly Review, vol. 5, 1855, pp. 561-572.— Sharpe's London Magazine, vol. 33, 1868, pp. 139-144.—Apple-ton's Journal, with portrait, by R. H. Stoddard, vol. 5, 1871, pp. 431-434.—Eclectic Magazine, with portrait, vol. 81, 1873, pp. 628, 629.—Catholic World, by J. L. Spalding, vol. 24, 1877, pp. 433-444.— Leisure Hour (with portrait), vol. 27, 1878, pp. 312-318. —Harper's New Monthly Magazine (with portrait), by H. P. Spofford, vol. 68, 1884, pp. 171-188.—Scribner's Monthly, by R. H. Stoddard, vol. 18, 1879, pp. 569-583.—Century Magazine, by E. C. Stedman, vol. 30, 1885, pp. 38-50.— Atlantic Monthly, by D. A. Wasson, vol. 13, 1864, pp. 331-338.—Longman's Magazine, by R. E. Prothero, vol. 9, 1887, pp. 182-189.—Good Words, by F. H. Underwood, vol. 28, 1887, pp. 29-34.—Critic, by J. H. Morse, vol. 11, 1887, pp. 307, 308.—Andover Review, vol. 9, 1888, pp. 86, 87.—Dial (Chicago), by M. B. Anderson, vol. 9, 1888, pp. 193-196.— Sunday Magazine, by Mary Harrison, Nov. 1892, pp. 766-768.—Westminster Review, by Mary Negreponte, Jan. 1893, pp. 7-11.—Century Magazine (with portrait), by Elizabeth S. Phelp, Jan. 1893, pp. 363-368.

——and American Poetry. Church Quarterly Review, vol. 30, 1890, pp. 160-171.

——and Curtis. Academy, by Walter Lewin, Sept. 17, 1892, pp. 237, 238.

——and his Writings. North American Review, vol. 79, 1854, pp. 31-52.

——and Marblehead. Chautauquan, by Margaret B. Wright, Sept. 1891, pp. 741-746.

——*and Tennyson.* Arena, by W. A. Fowler, vol. 7, 1892, pp. 1-11.

——*at Amesbury.* Critic, by Harriet P. Spofford, Nov. 1, 1884, pp. 205, 206.

—— *Autobiography of.* Critic, vol. 12, 1888, pp. 59, 60.

——*Devotional Poems of.* Sunday at Home, by Lily Watson, 1891, pp. 612-615.

——*Eightieth Birthday of* (poem). Atlantic Monthly, by Frances L. Mace, vol. 61, 1888, p. 111.

——*Home Ballads and Poems.* North British Review, vol. 34, 1861, pp. 210-216.—Athenæum, Aug. 31, 1861, pp. 276, 277; same article, Littell's Living Age, vol. 71, 1876, pp. 90-92.

——*In Memory of* (poem). Atlantic Monthly, by Oliver Wendell Holmes, vol. 70, 1892, pp. 648, 649.

——*in Prose.* Democratic Review, vol. 17, 1845, pp. 115-126.

——*In War Time and other Poems.* North American Review, by J. R. Lowell, vol. 98, 1864, pp. 290-292.

——*King's Missive.* Dial, by F. F. Browne, vol. 1, 1881, pp. 236, 237.

——*Lays of my Home.* Christian Examiner, vol. 35, 1843, pp. 261-263.—North American Review, vol. 57, 1843, pp. 509, 510.

——*Life Sketch of.* Western Monthly, by H. Stanton, vol. 3, 1870, pp. 298-302.

——*Mogg Megone.* North American Review, by C. C. Felton, vol. 44, 1837, pp. 547-549.

——*Notes of his Life and of his Friendships.* Harper's Magazine (Illustrated), by Annie Fields, Feb. 1893, pp. 338-339.

——*Obituary Notice of.* Athenæum, Sept. 10, 1892, pp. 354, 355.

——*Old Portraits and Modern Sketches.* North American Review, by C. C. Felton, vol. 70, 1850, pp. 524, 525.

——*Poems.* Methodist Quarterly, by R. Allyn, vol. 40, 1858, pp. 72-92.—Boston Quarterly Review, vol. 1, 1838, pp. 21-33.— Universalist Quarterly, vol. 6, 1849, pp. 142-160.—Athenæum, Feb. 18, 1882, pp. 215, 216.— Catholic Presbyterian, by A. Macleod, vol. 8, 1882, pp. 42-46.

—— ——*Local Associations of.* Harper's New Monthly Magazine, by G. M. White, vol. 66, 1882, pp. 353-367.

——*Snow-Bound.* North American Review, by J. R. Lowell, vol. 102, 1866, pp. 631, 632.

——*the Quaker Poet.* Gentleman's Magazine, by T. C. Hadden, vol. 273, 1892, pp. 408-417.— Leisure Hour, by E. F. Mayo, Jan. 1893, pp. 164-170.

—— *Talk with.* Lakeside Monthly, by R. Collyer, vol. 5, 1871, pp. 365-367.

——*Tent on the Beach.* Nation, by J. R. Dennett, vol. 4, 1867, pp. 186, 187.

——*Underwood's Life of.* Athenæum, July 26, 1884, pp. 106-108.

——*Vision of Echard.* Canadian Monthly, vol. 14, 1878, pp. 629-631.

——*Visit to birthplace of.* Scribner's Monthly, vol. 4, 1872, pp. 581-583.

——*Voices of Freedom.* New Englander, vol. 6, 1848, pp. 58-66.

——*Work of.* Chautauquan, by Emma J. Haney, vol. 25, 1892 pp. 79-81.

——*Writings of.* Athenæum, Oct. 12, 1889, pp. 479-480.—Spectator, Oct. 26, 1889, pp. 555, 556.

V. CHRONOLOGICAL LIST OF WORKS.

Legends of New England .	1831
Moll Pitcher . . .	1832
Literary Remains of J. G. C. Brainard . . .	1832
Justice and Expediency .	1833
Mogg Megone . . .	1836
Letters from John Quincy Adams to his Constituents [*Edited*] . .	1837
Poems written during the progress of the Abolition Question . . .	1837
Ballads, etc. . . .	1838
Lays of my Home, and other Poems . . .	1843
The Stranger in Lowell .	1845
Voices of Freedom . .	1846
The Supernaturalism of New England . .	1847
Leaves from Margaret Smith's Journal . .	1849
Poems [Complete edition]	1849
Songs of Labor and other Poems	1850
Old Portraits and Modern Sketches . . .	1850
The Chapel of the Hermits and other Poems . .	1853
A Sabbath Scene . .	1853
Literary Recreations and Miscellanies . .	1854
The Panorama and other Poems	1856
Poems [Complete edition] .	1857
Home Ballads, Poems and Lyrics	1860
In War Time and other Poems	1863
Snow-Bound . . .	1866
Prose Works (2 vols.) .	1866
Maud Muller . . .	1867
National Lyrics . .	1867
The Tent on the Beach .	1867
Among the Hills and other Poems	1869
Ballads of New England .	1870
Miriam and other Poems .	1871
Child Life ; a collection of Poems [*Edited*] . .	1872
The Pennsylvania Pilgrim and other Poems. .	1872
The Journal of John Woolman [*Edited*] . .	1872
Child Life in Prose [*Edited*]	1874
Mabel Martin and other Poems	1874
Hazel Blossoms . . .	1875
Songs of Three Centuries [*Edited*] . . .	1876
The Vision of Echard and other Poems . . .	1878
The King's Missive and other Poems . . .	1881
Letters of Lydia Maria Child [*Edited*] . .	1883
The Bay of Seven Islands and other Poems . .	1883
Poems of Nature . .	1886
Saint Gregory's Guest and recent Poems . . .	1886
Writings (*Riverside Edition,* in 7 vols) . .	1888-89